exploring HEAVENLY PLACES

Gates, Doors, and the Grid

VOLUME 3

PAUL L. COX
BARBARA KAIN PARKER

EXPLORING HEAVENLY PLACES
Gates, Doors, and the Grid
Volume 3

Paul L. Cox and Barbara Kain Parker

Aslan's Place Publications
9315 Sagebrush
Apple Valley, CA 92308
760-810-0990

www.aslansplace.com

Unless otherwise noted, all scripture quotations are from the New King James Version of the Bible. Copyright © 1979, 1980, 1982 by Thomas Nelson, Inc., publishers. Used by permission.

Scripture quotations marked ESV are from The Holy Bible, English Standard Version. Copyright © 2001 by Crossway Bibles, a publishing ministry of Good News Publishers.

Scripture quotations marked NASB are from the New American Standard Bible. Copyright © 1960, 1962, 1963, 1968, 1971, 1972, 1973, 1975, 1977, 1995 by The Lockman Foundation.

Scripture quotations marked NIV are from the Holy Bible, New International Version®, NIV®. Copyright ©1973, 1978, 1984, 2011 by Biblica, Inc.® Used by permission.

Greek definitions are derived from Strong's Greek Concordance.
Hebrew definitions are derived from Strong's Hebrew Concordance.

Copyright 2015 by Paul Cox and Barbara Kain Parker
All rights reserved.
Cover design and layout by Brodie Schmidtke
ISBN # 978-1-63452-015-7
Printed in the United States of America

TABLE OF CONTENTS

INTRODUCTION

Those of us who have been in the church since childhood remember praying this prayer every week. Even as a Baptist pastor, I (Paul) would lead the congregation to pray:

> *In this manner, therefore, pray: Our Father in heaven, hallowed be Your name. Your kingdom come. Your will be done on earth as it is in heaven. Give us this day our daily bread. And forgive us our debts, as we forgive our debtors. And do not lead us into temptation, but deliver us from the evil one. For Yours is the kingdom and the power and the glory forever. Amen.*[1]

Just before the Lord came in power to our Baptist church, I had taught a series of messages on the Lord's Prayer. In the final sermon of the series I preached that His Kingdom is one of power and glory, never knowing that in the following days I would begin to experience Him in a way I had never dreamed possible. At the end of the sermon I gave an invitation that I'd not anticipated throughout the days of preparation for that Sunday's sermon. I invited the people to come forward if they wanted to receive all that God wanted them to have. I was shocked, first that I said it, and then even more so when everyone came forward except for one visitor. Just four months later, I led my first deliverance session and then began experiencing the Power of God. The Lord had heard the people and accepted their plea to receive all that He wanted for them—things they said they wanted. The tragedy is that they did not recognize Him on the day of His visitation,[2] and eventually one-half of the church rejected what the entire church had asked for on that Sunday in May.

It is not just the phrase in the Lord's Prayer, "the power and the glory," to which the Lord has responded. He is also showing us that His will must first be done in Heaven before it happens here on Earth. We must explore the heavenly places through His leadership, taking back what has been given away to the enemy. As we do so, victory can first be secured in heavenly places, and then reflected here on Earth.

Though we often ritually recite the Lord's Prayer, there seems to be extreme resistance to the idea of exploring heavenly places. We, as leaders, have failed to explore them under the Lordship of Jesus Christ, and we have not encouraged those under our care to reach out to conquer the heavenly places so that they can experience a victorious life. This is not a new phenomenon in our 21st century world. In the first century, Jesus had issues with the religious people of Israel:

> But woe to you, scribes and Pharisees, hypocrites! For you shut up the king-dom of heaven against men; for you neither go in yourselves, nor do you allow those who are entering to go in.[3]

This third book in the *Exploring Heavenly Places* series examines in an elemen-tary way the nature of the heavenly places as a system of spheres, grids, gates, doors and kingdoms. We will also provide evidence that when His will is done in these places, there is a direct result in our earthly physical realm.

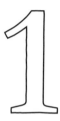

CHAPTER ONE

Highways to Holiness

Outside of Fairbanks, Alaska in the 1990s, I (Paul) was praying through a church building with the pastor. No matter how much we prayed we could not seem to get a breakthrough. But then I had the impression to feel for lines running through the worship center, and discerned lines running the length and width of the room like a grid.[1] I invited the pastor to cut these lines, and immediately the spiritual atmosphere of the worship center changed. I realized the importance of understanding these lines, and so the journey to discover what they were commenced, and I soon learned that in the secular world they are called 'ley lines'.

It is said that the word 'ley' comes from the Saxon word for cleared glade. In *The Ley Guide,* Paul Devereux and Ian Thompson quote from the *Concise Oxford English Dictionary* that the word 'ley' can be linked to 'lea' meaning a 'track of open ground'.

Alfred Watkins (1855-1935), a locally well-known and respected Herefordshire businessman discovered ley lines on June 30, 1921. While looking at a map for interesting features, noticed a straight line that passed over hilltops through various points of interest, all of which were ancient. At the time of his discovery, Watkins had no theory about alignments, but on that June afternoon he saw 'in a flash' a whole pattern of lines stretching across the landscape. Four years later, in 1925, he described his vision in a book titled, *The Old Straight Track:*

> Imagine a chain stretched from mountain peak to mountain peak, as far as the eye could reach, and laid out until it reached the 'high places' of the Earth at a number of ridges, banks, and knolls. Then visualize a mound, circular earthwork, or clump of trees, planted on these high points, and in low points in the valley other mounds ringed around with water to be seen from a distance. Then great standing stones brought to mark the way at intervals, and on a bank leading up to a mountain ridge or down to a ford the track cut deep so as to form a guiding notch on the skyline as you come up...Here and there, at two ends of the way, a beacon fire used to lay out the track. With ponds dug on the line, or streams banked up into 'flashes' to form reflecting points on the beacon track so that it might be checked when at least once a year the beacon was fired on the traditional day. All these are on the sighting line.

Watkins surmised that these straight tracks, or ley lines as he called them at first, were the remnants of prehistoric trading routes. He went on to associate ley lines with the Greek god, Hennes (the Roman, Mercury; and the Norse, Woden), who was the god of communication and of boundaries, the winged messenger, and the guide to travelers on unknown paths. Watkins identified Hennes-Mercury with the chief god of the Druids.

The identification of leys as ancient traders' routes was as far as Watkins was prepared to go, despite the fact that numerous ley lines traveled up steep hillsides. Speculation as to their meaning and purpose continued after Watkins' death in 1935.

NASA surveys have found paths running through the mountainous rainforest of Costa Rica. These paths, which follow relatively straight lines despite the difficult terrain, have been examined at ground level and have been dated to AD500-1200. Investigators discovered that the paths are 'death roads', and are still used for carrying corpses to burial, and also for transporting volcanic stone used in the construction of tombs and cemetery walls.

Are there any biblical references to these ley lines? Before we look at any references to ley lines I believe there is a biblical principle we must understand, which is that the enemy cannot create anything. He can only pervert or corrupt what the Lord has already created. If that is true, then is there a righteous understanding to these lines?

Isaiah 35:8-9 may give us an indication of these righteous lines:

> *And a highway will be there; it will be called the Way of Holiness. The unclean will not journey on it; it will be for those who walk in that Way; wicked fools will not go about on it. No lion will be there, nor will any ferocious beast get up on it; they will not be found there. But only the redeemed will walk there. (NIV)*

Note that there is a highway that the righteous will travel on, and the unrighteous are not permitted on this passageway. I would suggest that there might be a secondary understanding to this passage. While the scripture would primarily refer to those humans who are redeemed, it may also suggest another type of highway, i.e. a horizontal spiritual highway. Incidentally, Jacob's ladder mentioned in Genesis may be a reference to a vertical highway. Perhaps the Lord has established these highways as locations of spiritual movement. Some have called them 'portals'. Psalm 16:6 also speaks of lines:

> *The boundary lines have fallen for me in pleasant places; surely I have a delightful inheritance. (NIV)*

The corruption of these lines by the enemy would give permission for the enemy to utilize the lines for evil purposes. Isaiah 34:11 may speak of this:

> *God will stretch out over Edom the measuring line of chaos and the plumb line of desolation. (NIV)*

This line of chaos could very easily refer to ley lines, and the plumb line of desolation could speak of what I call up-shoots, or vertical connecting lines between horizontal layers of ley lines. Could the enemy use these lines for communication and travel?

If it is true that the enemy has corrupted what the Lord had intended for good, then how did this happen?

When Adam and Eve sinned, they turned creation over to the enemy. Perhaps part of what was turned over was these lines. Romans 8:19-21 speaks of a time when we as the children of God will take back for the Lord what the enemy has captured:

The creation waits in eager expectation for the children of God to be revealed. For the creation was subjected to frustration, not by its own choice, but by the will of the one who subjected it, in hope that the creation itself will be liberated from its bondage to decay and brought into the freedom and glory of the children of God. (NIV)

When we give our lives to Jesus Christ, we are given back authority over creation. However, we must exercise that authority and take back what was given to the enemy, and we can again establish the highways of holiness by asking the Lord to purify these lines. I do this by walking the length and width of a house and/or property, cutting off the contamination of the enemy. Note that slight change in terminology—once we understood that the ley lines are God's creation, we began cutting off the contamination rather than cutting the lines themselves as we did initially. Incidentally, the Lord may actually position us at certain places so that we can take back specific areas. Acts 17:26 tells us that we are to establish His Kingdom where we live:

From one man he made every nation of men, that they should inhabit the whole earth; and he determined the times set for them and the exact places where they should live. (NIV)

As time passed, the Lord continued giving us new insight into ley lines.

February 9, 2009, from Persis Tiner:[2]

Networking, networking
Many the lines, which are not divine
Many the doors open to evil
Through these communication lines

Beware; beware
Be prepared; be prepared
The battle is brewing
Be not deceived

The enemy has prepared

To tap into these lines
Ley lines, ley lines
New lines to old lines
Time lines, key lines
Wrong lines for My lines

My lines are pure lines
That will get the job done
These lines are his, Satan's, lines
To have his bad fun

Gather the elders
Gather them soon
Gather at AP (Aslan's Place)
Just past the full moon

I'll give you new wisdom
Revelation to impart
Do this and hurry
As you seek My pure heart

March 16, 2009, from Persis Tiner:

All around, all around
Danger, danger
All around

Entrapped, entrapped
You've been entrapped
By lies and deceits
From near and from far

Cleanse the lines
Ley lines, ley lines
Cleanse the lines
Phone lines, phone lines

Wires, wires
Are also involved

Cleanse the signals
Before you fall

Sneaky is the plan
And wide is the scope
The enemy has devised
To stop up the flow

In the heart of the matter
Foundations are involved
Deep, deep, these cracks go
And, yes, they prevent My pure flow

The flow of My spirit
The flow of My grace
The flow to bring Heaven
To My heavenly place

You have the answers
You have the keys
Take counsel; take counsel
Many pieces you need

Remember the words
That you've heard recently
Change and new wineskins
Change and new sounds
Don't chose the old ways
To bring forth new birth

You've now seen the enemy
You can be prepared
Shoot him down at the pass
Mow him over and laugh

April 10, 2009, from Persis Tiner regarding a meeting in Georgia:

There is a roar throughout the land
"Georgia, Georgia,"

It does proclaim
The armies are coming
Coming to proclaim
The Way, the Way of the Lord

Clean off the ley lines
The roads and the hills
The Lord's Army is coming
To make a great kill

The year of His vengeance
His vengeance is here
New sounds and vibrations
His army to bring
Bring for His glory
Bring for the King

Bring healing; bring health
Bring peace and new hope
Restore breaches and walls
Restore words and great wealth

Restoring, renewing, revitalizing
Reversing the curses
Of sooo many years
Bringing the news of great hope
The armies are here

Here to restore order
Open heavens anew
Over Georgia, sweet Georgia
Holding My bride sooo true

August 9, 2010, from Larry Pearson[3] in Collingwood, Canada:

Bringing you into new realms of revelation. Step in; step in to behold...this path you have not walked before. Take My hand as we take the land, as we gather up the ancient lines... As we gather we shall find the gold. We will find the gold as we gather. I am about to unlock the head. Quarter by quarter, line by line; your foe does not like this. He has been found out. It is time to focus beyond your default, beyond your battle. Step into the holy intention. Not by might, nor by power, but by My Spirit. Deeper revelation about the communication; the communication has been defiled…It is coming from the entities on the lines. It has been a generational hop. It has hopped off of one generation to another. It is connected to the void, the false universe…

April 17, 2012, from Persis Tiner:

It's the convergence of evil
It sits on the grid
Where the doors and the gates
The ley lines and paths
Have been established by evil

Set way back in time
It's evil; it's evil
It's high-level evil
Born of the fall
Empowered by Lucifer
Mingled with blood from the altars of hell
Waiting to be exposed by the church of this time

Unraveling, exposing
Layer upon layer
The time of its disposing
Is now, yes, it is now

So, what is the practical application for all of this? We have witnessed some amazing results when contaminated ley lines were cleansed.

Donna and I have a friend who had just built a new home. Night after night she found it impossible to sleep. In desperation, she asked us to come over to the house to see what we discerned. As we walked into the master bedroom, I felt a large ley line running across her bed. We had her cut off the contamination, and that night she was able to sleep for the first time in her new bedroom. A Swiss pastor and his wife tell an amazing story about their discovery of ley lines in a German home. They had been invited to pray for a crippled woman in a German village who had been stooped over for many years. As they prayed for her, they learned that there were witches living on each side of her home, and then discerned a large ley line running through her house. As they broke the contamination, she immediately stood up straight. She had been healed!

Perhaps freedom in your home is tied to breaking off the evil on these lines. Seek the Lord and see what He would have you do.

CHAPTER TWO

Introducing the Grid

As our understanding of ley lines developed, God also began introducing us to the concept of the grid, beginning with a dream from Dale Shannon[1] in May 2006, in which Paul was speaking to her from Heaven. She could see a grid, and Paul was instructed to go into it and disconnect something. From that point, many others began seeing grids in dreams and visions, one of my own being that I was looking up at what appeared to be crisscrossed electrical power lines, just as one might see in the physical realm.

As always, all that we are seeing and learning must conform to scripture or it cannot be God's truth. Rob Gross[2] developed a PowerPoint presentation for his church in Kaneohe, Hawaii called *The Power of God (Understanding the Grid)*. Part of that is shared here in outline form in order to lay the biblical foundation for ongoing revelation:

I. **Power Verses**

    A. *You will receive power when the Holy Spirit has come upon you.* [3]

    B. *For I am not ashamed of the gospel of Christ: for it is the power of God unto salvation to everyone that believeth.* [4]

C. *The same power that raised this Christ from the dead is living in you.* [5]

D. *For I will not venture to speak of anything except what Christ has accomplished through me to bring the Gentiles to obedience—by word and deed, by the power of signs and wonders, by the power of the Spirit of God.* [6]

E. *For the preaching of the cross is to them that perish foolishness; but unto us which are saved it is the power of God.* [7]

F. *And I was with you in weakness and in fear and much trembling, and my speech and my message were not in plausible words of wisdom, but in the demonstration of the Spirit and power.* [8]

G. *That your faith should not stand in the wisdom of men, but in the power of God.* [9]

H. *For the kingdom of God is not in word, but in power.* [10]

I. *Our gospel came to you not only in word, but also in power and in the Holy Spirit and with full conviction.* [11]

II. **What is the power of God? It is:**

A. God's supernatural, creative ability to make things happen, such as:

1. Heal the sick.
2. Set people free from spiritual and emotional bondages.
3. Perform miracles.
4. Proclaim the gospel to those who don't know Jesus, with signs and wonders following.
5. God's unquenchable love for people in action.

III. **Where is the power?**

A. It's on the pathway:

1. *And a highway shall be there, and it shall be called the Way of Holiness; the unclean shall not pass over it. It shall belong to those who walk on the way; even if they are fools, they shall not go astray.* [12]

2. *In those days John the Baptist came preaching in the wilderness of Judea, "Repent, for the kingdom of heaven is at hand." For this is he who was spoken of by the prophet Isaiah when he said, "The voice of one crying in the wilderness: 'Prepare the way of the Lord; make straight His paths'".* [13]

3. *These twelve Jesus sent out, instructing them, "Go nowhere among the Gentiles and enter no town of the Samaritans, but rather go to the lost sheep of the house of Israel. And proclaim as you go, saying, 'The kingdom of God is at hand.' Heal the sick, raise the dead, cleanse the lepers, cast out demons".* [14]

B. The pathway is like an electrical grid.

IV. What is an electrical grid?

A. It is a transmission system for electrical power.

B. In the spiritual realm we stand in the midst of a three dimensional pathway or power grid in the heavenly places.

V. In military terms the grid refers to airways, highways, lines of communication, waterways:

A. In the military, whoever controls the airways, highways, lines of communication, and waterways controls the war.

B. We are in a war with the enemy for grid supremacy.

VI. In the spiritual realm, the grid is:

A. Point to point, as in Heaven to Earth or vice versa.

B. Point to point over time, as from one generation to the next.

C. Point to point as in the release of God's power to His children.

VII. Why does the enemy want control of the grid? Because whoever controls the pathway in the heavenly places controls which kingdom is established on Earth—the Kingdom of God, or the kingdom of darkness.

VIII. Gates, doors and the grid:

A. Wherever the grid lines intersect on the pathway there is a gate.

B. Gates connect the grid lines in the heavenly places.

C. Gates are entry points into the heavenly places, while doors are entry points within the heavenly places.

D. Gates were the primary entry points into ancient cities and served as civic centers where business, government and spiritual matters were conducted. If a foreign enemy wanted to capture a city, he would come against its gate.

E. Likewise, in the spiritual realm, when the enemy comes against God's people, His goal is to capture the gates.

IX. What happened at the Fall?

A. The enemy gained control of the heavenly places.

B. The enemy gained control of the pathways of the grid.

C. The enemy gained control of the gates and doors.

X. Why does the enemy constantly seek to establish his kingdom in the heavenly realms? He wants access!

XI. What happened at the cross?

A. Christ redeemed and regained control of the heavenly places.

B. Christ redeemed and regained control of the pathway or grid.

C. Christ redeemed and regained control of the gates and doors.

XII. Because of what Jesus accomplished on the cross, we are able to retake the pathway, or grid, from the enemy and prepare the way of the Lord.

XIII. Gates, doors, doorways scriptures:

A. *I will surely bless you, and I will surely multiply your offspring as the stars of heaven and as the sand that is on the seashore. And your offspring shall possess the gate of his enemies.* [15]

B. *And they blessed Rebekah and said to her, "Our sister, may you become thousands of ten thousands, and may your offspring possess the gate of those who hate him".* [16]

C. *And he was afraid and said, "How awesome is this place! This is none other than the house of God and the gate of heaven."* [17]

D. *And he said to him, "Truly, truly, I say to you, you will see heaven opened, and the angels of God ascending and descending on the Son of man."* [18]

E. *Go through, go through the gates; prepare the way for the people; build up, build up the highway; clear it of stones; lift up a signal over the peoples".* [19]

F. *Lift up your heads O gates! And be lifted up, O ancient doors, that the King of glory may come in.* [20]

G. *Blessed are those who listen to me, watching daily at my doors, waiting at my door-way.* [21]

XIV. Behind many doors, doorways and gates on the grid is a demonic kingdom filled with belief systems, lies and mindsets that keep individuals and nations in bondage. Some closed doors are access points into heavenly places that should be opened.

XV. What are the lines on the pathway or grid? In the natural, grid lines are transmission networks that transfer electrical energy from a power plant to its customers.

XVI. Grid lines have transformers, and a transformer is:

A. An electrical device that takes energy of one voltage and changes it to another voltage.

B. A power distribution system that changes high voltage into lower voltage.

XVII. What happens when we restore the grid? The enemy's strongholds will fall and people will be saved, delivered, healed and discipled.

CHAPTER THREE

Ongoing Revelation of the Grid

During a ministry school in October 2008, an angel arrived with a message and one of the participants delivered it:

> Courage. Have courage my son. For the times and the seasons will begin to unfold as My glory rises up from the well…I will send powers[1] to help you; trees of righteousness, the planting of the Lord. They will be like power lines to set up a new grid, even around this city, for I would banish the power of the ley lines. And I would restructure the grid because I want a new voltage to flow. I am going to change the voltage and you are going to carry more power.

In September 2009, a friend of Aslan's Place dreamed:

> This dream was different than most of my dreams in that I didn't feel like I was observing but was participating. I began to be jettisoned from Earth to outer space. It was dark, but not pitch black, and I sensed that the stars gave off a faint light. It was fast and instant. I found myself trying to balance on grid lines that could only be seen

with my spiritual eyes. They reminded me of the lights used in the aisle of a plane, except they ran in parallel lines in groups of three. They were not perpendicular to each other, but not random either, and were symmetrically placed.

Paul recalls a ministry school in Las Vegas, Nevada on July 19, 2010, when they discerned the ungodly fourth grid (upper right hand quadrant of the brain) created by the enemy. (Note: the four quadrants are also present in other contexts, such as the heart. The brain is just one example.)

The morning started off with the delivery of a spiritual scroll, which was read by Jana Green:[2]

> His eyes are looking. They are going back and forth throughout the Earth, looking not at the outward appearance but at the heart to see the hearts that are perfect before Him. He desires to have a people He can look at and honor, a people whose heart is true before Him and contains the desires of His heart.
>
> He wants to give the secret and hidden things that were written in days of old but were held back…It was not the time then, but He desires now to give them to those whose hearts are ready, for His people need them for the time of the end.
>
> The grids that we've been talking about are not just grids, but are nets to catch the fish. Everything that He is doing we are to take, and work with those nets and bring in the fish. His heart is big. He has room for everyone. He is not willing that anyone perish. He desires that each of us take what we've been given to bring in the fish that they might do the same.

As the discernment and exploration regarding what the Lord was doing that day unfolded, there was much back-and-forth in terms of comments, questions, prayers, etc. At one point, Dale Shannon said:

> God is building a foundation. We put rebar in the foundation and pour cement and build a church. The Lord was building upon the Apostles and Prophets as the foundation, as the grid. God is building a new foundation, taking away the old foundation.

Paul then shared Ephesians 2:20 and Zechariah 4:9, noting that the foundation that is mentioned may refer to the grid:

Paul continued:

> The foundation of the chessboard is the 8 x 8 grid. You stand with Melchizedek on the chessboard. We got put on the foundation that wisdom has built. It is a cube in a cube in a cube. I think it is the Holy of Holies. It is a dimensional grid; it is a multi-dimensional chessboard. This is a worldwide power; this is the Righteous Power established in the grid. It is the righteous web. It is a power grid… the chessboard is called the trading floor in the Masonic.

Here is part of a much longer word delivered by Lewis Crompton[3] that was mostly specific to Las Vegas.

> I have been gracious and worked upon their foundation. I work within their regime, within their control for I am gracious and I am humble, but I will be free and once again I will move in power that they cannot contain, and though they can shut down one they cannot shut down an army. If they kill one, I will raise up two; if they kill two I will raise up four; if they kill four I will raise up eight. This is a new beginning. They try to stop Me moving to and fro throughout the nations [but] I am no longer bound by geography. I am not bound to the Earth; the Earth is bound to Me. I will walk across the Earth in the hearts of My people. I am grounded in their hearts and they are hidden in Mine; heart to heart, face-to-face, worshipping in spirit and truth; for I bring about a day of triumph, and now it begins… Joseph is coming. Dominion rule is coming. Dominion must be taken. It will not be given. Take hold of that which Christ took hold of you for. We are no longer in the nursery but you still need to color outside the lines. Do not be limited to that which was drawn for you. Be limitless as I am limitless. Be holy as I am holy. Be perfect as I am perfect. Can I not do all things through Christ who strengthens you, who intercedes for you? I am sending perfection to My bride, for only those who don't believe the lie will receive her. For many have said perfection is not possible this side of eternity. Where are you living? For I have placed eternity in your hearts, and I will write My law on your heart, for this is the place that you live from, not from your mind but from your heart because you live from

eternity, from the heavenly places. You will not be perfect if you live on the Earth but you now live in Heaven because you do not live on the Earth. You live on the firm foundation that is Jesus Christ who is seated at the right hand of the Father. You are not of the world but of the divine nature. You are in the world but not of it.

As the session ended, Dale Shannon saw the grid as a square, getting higher and higher and higher, growing, and looking like a blue diamond. She heard:

And you will shine. You are part of the structure and you are shining like the diamonds. My radiance; you reflect My radiance. It is not you they see, but Me and you because I am transferring authority to you now, [transferring] the Kingdom to you now because you have not asked for titles and positions...and My mandate is to take the land in spirit and in truth and love and humility. Encourage one another. You are not competing but you are working together on My team, joined together, knit together. They are part of a structure and you are part of the structure. The transference is being recorded in a heavenly scroll, the establishment of the structure." At this point, Dale saw a Godly structure that looked like a rectangle with a diamond iridescent blue shine, and made up of people.

During a meeting in Collingwood, Canada on August 8, 2010, Mimi Lowe[4] delivered the word:

There is a universal time clock that is out of sync. Other adjustments have to be made to bring you back into right time and space. You cannot just adjust one and not the other. Rolling back time. Rolling it back. Like pieces of a jigsaw puzzle, you fixed one but you must fix the others. There is a correlation between time, space, color; all these are intertwined; all are part of the grid, part of the network.

In November 12, 2010, Paul observed:

We've been in Zechariah 4 yesterday and today, which is about the foundation of the temple. Notice the phrase, "the stone in the hand of Zerubbabel" (NKJ says plumb line, but it is really a stone). I can feel the stone in my left hand. It seems to be a cube and the flow from the seven eyes of the Lord on us seems to go through that stone. It seems that stone is part of the crystal sea, which seems to be the grid.

Dena Plantage[5] then shared a dream:

> I am standing in a temple but there are no walls or even a roof over-
> head. It is falling and is ruined. Many, many people are being forced
> to wait in a line. There are others that aren't part of this line for they
> are the overseers (who seem to be an organized evil) for the process
> of binding people to this line. There seems to be a box that everyone
> is being thrown into by force and they lay on top of each other, cry-
> ing in torment and pain and suffering. Bound and unable to move,
> below them comes up sections like metal walls. It would look like
> a cube that is multiplying, and then again there are sections of metal
> walls that come from another direction, which eventually cubes ev-
> erything off into pieces of small squares. As I stand there in horror,
> I am feeling that there is something that could be done about this. I
> really feel that this is a wake up call to us all that we are to stand to-
> gether. We are at war against what the scriptures are describing to us;
> there are things unseen to the human eye, and we are to learn spiritual
> discernment. Those who are in Christ have liberating authority over
> these powers. Paul wrote about a lot of this in the scriptures.

> *Finally, my brethren, be strong in the Lord and in the power of His
> might. Put on the whole armor of God, that you may be able to stand
> against the wiles of the devil. For we do not wrestle against flesh and
> blood, but against principalities, against powers, against the rulers of
> the darkness of this age, against spiritual hosts of wickedness in the
> heavenly places. Therefore take up the whole armor of God, that you
> may be able to withstand in the evil day, and having done all, to stand.*[6]

Dena also prepared a picture of how she sees the grid:

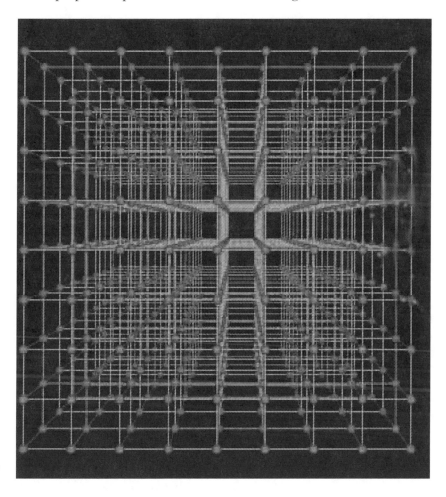

On August 28, 2011, Persis Tiner heard, "Storm troopers, forerunners, front guard, spear headers, timely, piercing, lightning is capable of bringing change, revelation, judgment & correction." Then she received the following rhyme:

Lightnings and thunderings
Come from above
Piercing the darkness
And bringing My love

Piercing the depths
So dark and so cruel

Setting free captives
And making them bold

Bringing deliverance and healing
To the sick and infirmed
Knocking out power grids
The enemy has formed
And setting free territories
To be free and so bold

Watch now and listen
The thunderings and lightnings to hear
Whether by spirit or
Whether by ear
Whether they be single or
Whether they be many
Appointed by God
To bring freedom to many

On October 15, 2011, Larry Pearson wrote:

While we were discussing the grid I was caught up into a vision (trance) in which I saw the King high and lifted up. The train of His robe is the grid that fills the whole universe. We are inside the fabric of His garments. I noticed there is some of it bunched up (crooked places) that are in need of being made straight by our ruling declarations to the enemies at the gates. The train of His robe fills all in all.

On July 10, 2013, Dawn Bray[7] described a picture, which she had a friend draw, of what she had been discerning on her head. Describing it, she wrote:

It is a sphere, inside one square on the grid. It is spinning and each square on the sphere is a panel that flips and both sides have code encrypted on them in the lines. It looks like shiny stones, we think because of the power/current on the lines. There are watchers at all 4 corners of the grid encasing the sphere. There is a constant sound like many waters coming from the sphere as it spins.

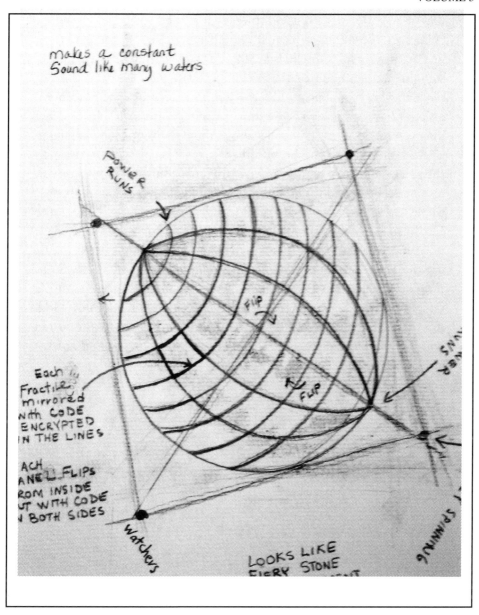

During a Discernment and Exploration session on September 27, 2014, Paul discerned the grid on one of the participants, said they were contaminated, and proceeded to both teach about and deal with the contamination.

Paul asked, "So what did we do? We ask the Lord to please clean these off—Lord, please clean off the lines. In Isaiah 35 they are called highways of holiness. Next, we ask the Lord to close all doors

27

that should be closed—Lord, please close all doors that should be closed and open all doors that should be opened so the gates will not be shut again. Grid lines are all over your body. Picture yourself standing in the middle of the grid...For those that say that this is not biblical; well, it is biblical and it is scientific. Brian Greene has a book called *The Fabric of the Cosmos* and you can go on YouTube and see his presentation where he talks about the dimensions. He is talking about string theory and he says these are gates, and you go through the gates into the dimensions. You can't make this stuff up...you can usually feel the grid inside the room. (He demonstrates) I think that there is a grid that is under the Earth, on the Earth and above the Earth, so everything is more confusing and complex than we think it is...But what's happening in Christ, you see, is that we are possessing the Kingdom of God...There is some reason why only we can do this. I believe that's why the fallen sons of God mated with the daughters of men; they wanted to take over the Kingdom of God, but they can't do it except through humanity. Because we are seated with Christ in heavenly places, I think that we are the ones that have access to the dimensions.

CHAPTER FOUR

Testimonials About the Grid

An intercessor's vision in September 2011, after a prayer session with Paul Cox:

> The Lord came up to me in the Spirit, took my hand and motioned for me to come with Him. So I took His hand and suddenly we were in this small tight tube-like thing—it was like a small elevator but had no tangible sides, top or bottom. We went lightning fast upwards, passing through the white clouds and sky, and then kept going up until we were in darkness with the stars and planets all around. We were in space, very high above the Earth, beyond where satellites go.
>
> All of sudden we stopped and just stood together suspended in darkness, with nothing around us it seemed; but suddenly, as if a veil were pulled back, I was in the midst of a room of many people, creatures, and angels who were all moving around, very busy. Then I heard, "command and control center." Everything and everybody had white, almost luminescent outlines, and weren't like people as we see them in the flesh. In other words, they didn't look solid like we do. But I could definitely see their faces, height, size, etc. There was equipment that looked like computers but they weren't. There

were things they were looking into that seemed to involve energy, almost like gyroscopes but different. I realized their equipment was far different than ours in that it involved more of what I would call life force or energy, or sinful or righteous powers. They seemed to be working with prayer, balancing and responding to good versus evil. They were also communicating with many places. I then saw many of these stations placed around the heavenlies—each one doing the same type of work.

They were very alert and in some ways tense, but not like us. I sensed that they were ready to close up shop and move at a moment's notice, and realized that being undetected by the enemy was key. I understood that this station moved around a lot. It was hidden for the moment from the enemy, but he could attack at any time. Then I looked out at the expanse of Heaven and then I saw the vast cosmos, and it was all in a cube-like grid with lines. I was reminded of Job 38:4-5:

> *Where were you when I laid the foundations of the earth? Tell Me, if you have understanding. Who set its measurements? Since you know. Or who <u>stretched out the line on it?</u> (NASB, emphasis mine)*

Wow, this blew me away! It was billions of miles of lines, never ending, going in all directions.

At this point I think I was wondering how everyone moved around when I saw something really wild. I watched an angel step into one of these lines, which seemed to be extremely small bands of light, but not really bright, and then suddenly disappear into the line. I knew he was on a mission to go somewhere but he did it on the grid line! He was IN the line and moving at the speed of light, going somewhere else to do who-knows-what, but he totally disappeared into the line!

I asked the Lord why he was showing this to me. He said He wanted me to know because He wanted me to understand how the spirit world works so that I could interact with it more intelligently. He is revealing the secrets of the Kingdom and of the spirit world at this time at a very quickened pace. It seemed like He had special missions and messages for me, particularly regarding America. He seemed very concerned, as did all the creatures in the station, about America.

By the way, it seemed as if there were humans at this station. Perhaps, and this is just an impression, they were those who had died and gone home before us and were now working in the Kingdom. In other words, angels aren't the only workers. Then I thought, do the unsaved work for the devil? This is something to think on perhaps.

One last thought as it regards spiritual warfare is that there were no weapons at this station or anywhere I could see. It seemed as if it was all about coordinating what we are doing on the Earth, and between Earth and the heavenlies. As if we're the ones with the weapons but the weapons were our words and our righteous acts. It seemed as if our holy living was a weapon! This was a new thought to me. I sort of expected some angelic missile base but really saw it was all about communication. Angels do carry swords and staffs I know, but it seems those are mostly to use against the enemy. In times past when I have seen them engage one another, they never really touch but move their opponent through authority, faith, righteousness, and by rank.

A testimony received in November 2014, following a deliverance session:

As the group was praying for me I saw myself trapped in a cube-like grid. Every time I would climb to the top and get close to escaping, the cube would rotate and I would end up at the bottom again. Eventually I got out. When I did, I grabbed the grid and slammed it into the ground. The grid shattered when it hit the ground. When it hit the ground (the ground was all dark and murky), the dark dissipated like a mist and I saw a demon-like figure looking up at me. Not only did I see the demon, but I also saw young women/girls standing spaced apart. It looked endless, like generations of young women. Now I am doing a lot better in the area of lust—waaaaaaaaayyyyyyy better.

Heather Baker's[1] testimony on January 14, 2015, regarding Handel's Messiah and the grid:

I had been listening to Dr. Paul Cox's YouTube videos on Star Wars. After the first video I noticed that I could see the grid he talks about. After watching the second video, I noticed I could see the grid pretty much any time I think about it. At bedtime, I have pictured myself in Heaven before the throne, on my face on the starry sky/crystal sea with the grid encompassing all of Heaven, time, and space. I feel safe there. It has helped me deal with the stress of watching my very intelligent parents lose their ability to deal with what is going on around them.

This morning, I was driving down the 405 to Laguna Woods to take my mom to a blood test. I had the second half of Handel's *Messiah* playing loudly on the CD in the car. As I drove, I became aware of a heavenly grid in front of me as the car went down the freeway. As I watched the grid while I drove, I noticed that I was seeing the music show up in the grid as waves of light. I have seen music before so this isn't new, but the format was different. Previously, I have seen the notes written in gold on staffs of gold in the air but now the music showed up as light waves and/or as sound waves portrayed in light passing through the spaces in the grid.

Since Handel's *Messiah* is written entirely using scripture, it was interesting to watch the effect on the grid. Every sound had some effect, some much stronger than others. It was beautiful to watch, and I began to notice some things. All the waves moved out from the source, which happened to be where I was seated in the car, and traveled to the distant parts of the grid. Different instruments created different sorts of waves; solo instruments sent out one wave; a section of the same instrument sent out a group of parallel waves, but when several sections of instruments were playing, there were several sets of parallel waves. Trumpets sent out waves that were shaped like the horns of trumpets, narrow at the beginning but growing wider the farther they went. They seemed to have a particular ability to penetrate the farther areas of the grid.

A solo human voice when the singer was singing a declaration was stronger than any of the instruments except a trumpet. If the human was singing a non-declarative praise text, the effect was less than with a declarative text. A section of human voices in unison sent out parallel waves, but stronger in intensity than the instruments. When all 4-voice sections sang in chorus, the effect filled a good portion of the grid.

During the Hallelujah Chorus, when the chorus sang, "The kingdom of this world is become the Kingdom of our Lord, and of His Christ, and He shall reign forever and ever," the effect was the most intense, because the passion and declarative intent of the text was having a stronger effect than the non-declarative texts. Also, the entire orchestra, including trumpets, was playing. The effect seemed to polarize the grid to a positive flow, not only of the music light waves, but along the pathways of the grid. This seemed to increase power and openness to the Spirit. It was intense and beautiful.

It seemed that unity of intent increased the brightness of the waves, which I took to mean increased strength. Passion increased the brightness. Victorious declarations sung in chorus by unified hearts had the greatest effect.

There seems to be something about how trumpets affect the grid, which may be why God chooses them or shofars to be His instrument of choice for certain occasions.

Maybe this is why many believers feel so led to worship and praise. It is having strong effects in unseen realms.

From Kelly Stark[2] on April 13, 2015:

Some time ago I had a vision in which I saw the Earth; and it had straight lines shooting all around it, connecting and crossing each other, with some creating a triangle shape in a very certain order. I was pulled up higher, where I saw the Earth with all the lines, and it looked like a giant crystal.

I'd heard about ley lines from my grandfather, but when I saw this I knew they were real, and I asked God in the vision, "Why did You let the devil create something so beautiful?" He answered, "He didn't make them, I did! And just like everything else I've made, the devil takes it and perverts it for his own purposes." I said, "Oh, I'm so glad You are the one that made it because it really is beautiful!"

After seeing this vision, I did some research and found that before they were called ley lines, different cultures had different names for them. The aborigines in Australia called them song or dream lines; the American Indians, spirit paths; the Celts, fairy paths; the Chinese, qi (or chi) energy lines; Tibetans and the occult called them dragon lines.

The image I saw that looked like a crystal is called an icosahedron, which has twelve points or vortices (vortex) that are in perfect alignment. There are twelve vortices, known in the occult as vile vortices, which are in perfect alignment with the icosahedron. They are the devils triangle (Japan), Hawaiian Islands, Bermuda Triangle, Himalayas (India), Algerian megaliths, Easter Island, Wharton Basin, offshore of Rio de Janeiro, Zimbabwe's ancient mines and structures (from Zimbabwe to Madagascar), Fiji and Loyalty Islands, North Pole and South Pole.

I had a VERY bizarre dream last night! I was in a place where there was so much noise and bizarre things going on. It was a like a million radios playing at once; loud, chaotic, and unnerving. In the dream, I realized I was dreaming, but then I 'popped' out of that dream into another dream, but it was the same thing again—noisy and bizarre, with nothing making sense! Again, I realized I was dreaming, and this happened ten times. I'm not kidding! The last time I realized I was dreaming I yelled out, "JESUS!" And the dream stopped, but I was still in it. And I said, "God what do you want me to know? What do you want me to do?" Then I was taken up on a mountain and saw the ley lines, and could see where they were corrupted, noisy, disrupted, and blocked. Like a radio wave trying to break through the noise, I heard God say, "Kelly, we need you keep the communication lines open so that the message can go through." And then I finally woke up!

Kelly's last dream had a very practical application. There is a specific location she had often visited, but on each occasion her discernment kicked in and she experienced terrible headaches, and felt as if her senses were being assaulted by the noise and the chaos. Recently, as she'd walked down a sidewalk there, she noticed a woman off to the side who was staring at her and chanting/praying an ungodly tongue. My (Barbara's) small group discussed all of this and prayed about it, and the Lord directed Kelly to go back to that location and cleanse the ley lines. Taking one other person, she did so shortly thereafter, and for the first time she had a sense of total peace and rest—and definitely no headache. Unlike every previous visit, she encountered people who were smiling and pleasant.

CHAPTER FIVE

A Confirming Vision

Growing up, I (Barbara) lived near the families of two of my dad's brothers and I was close to a couple of cousins who were about my age. As my younger siblings began arriving, so did younger cousins—all of whom we considered the 'little kids'. It's amazing how distant five or six years seem during our formative years, and how such age differences shrink into insignificance as adults.

Crystal was one of the little kids so we quickly lost touch with after my family moved away when I was seventeen. Many years later, around 2009, my cousin started calling occasionally and we'd talk awhile, but still didn't know one another well. Eventually though, we discovered that we are both passionate about God in a way that many others in our extended family are not; and a spiritual bond began to form. As time went by, she began sharing some of the visions the Lord had been giving her, and Crystal Kain Ross has now become a trusted prophetic voice at Aslan's Place.

In September 2007, Jesus began taking Crystal into the heavens where He introduced her to the power grid. Following is a compilation of some of those visions, all of which we were unaware of until April 2014, yet it parallels so many of the words we have received over the years extremely well.

The Vision Begins—the Placement of the Power Grid

It was the middle of the day. I was wide-awake, but suddenly saw a vision before me, as if looking at a hologram movie. Yet at the same time, I was not only looking at it but was in it and experiencing it with all my senses.

Immediately upon entering into prayer, I was up in the heavens with Jesus. I looked down, and far below I saw what I knew to be the circle of our planet Earth. It appeared as brilliant blue and was scattered with fluffy clouds, the oceans being distinct from the landmass.

Then I looked again and saw a massive gossamer patchwork of light coming down from above us. It looked like a living quilt of almost transparent light, except that it appeared to be thousands of miles across. It was moving, pulsating, and full of much of the Spirit's activity. Each section of this grid was dotted out with exacting squares in the measurement of what I was told were celestial stadia.

The living grid-quilt was so incredibly beautiful. It defies my ability to describe. It was obviously something created in Heaven for the Earth, and for its benefit. There were mighty angels holding the four corners and points in-between, flying with it. As they came past us with the huge lighted gossamer quilt, I heard amazing angel music and accompanying celestial orchestras. The air was thick with a very heavy-yet-light fragrance, infused with much of the Spirit's power and much joy.

I wondered how power and joy could have a fragrance, but in this realm of Heaven I am discovering that many things have a very distinct and glorious fragrance.

The mighty angels carrying the power-grid-quilt flew past us and down in swift fashion to Earth. They poised themselves high above the stratosphere and atmosphere, and when the position was just right, they let go of the corners. And there it laid, poised, ready, and seeming to wait—it seemed to float in place momentarily, and then it was anchored with lighted spikes into the air so that it would stay in its place.

I couldn't conceive of how the square power-grid-quilt would fit the round

Earth without overlap, but as it was positioned above, and started to settle down around the circle of the Earth, it suddenly and perfectly became the exact outer dimensions of the outer sphere beyond the Earth's atmosphere.

Jesus began to speak to me about this amazing sight, "This is the power grid which covers the Earth. It has been in place since the time of the creation of Adam, but I have taken you back with Me in a journey to that time so that you could see its placement at the beginning."

I asked, "What do the separate, distinct and measured celestial stadia sections mean?"

Jesus answered, "The sections are measured in celestial stadia for purposes of identification and order. These function much like the boundaries of states in your country. They separate areas of land, much as rivers and seas define the edges and borders of the countries on the Earth. Each section is named and numbered, although at this time you do not need to know these details—they are used for the inner functions of the heavenly workers. You, along with many others, have asked Me to reveal the deep and secret things, and I am giving you, and those who are seeking these deep things, My divine revelations now. These revelations are not for the sake of acquiring knowledge only, but are for use in ministry, intercession and effective prayer. Those who minister in these last days need to be informed about the deep and secret workings. I run the inner workings of My Kingdom much like the earthly military. There are levels of station and position, both with earthly and celestial ranks. In the higher ranks of earthly ministry, there comes a time when certain inside infor- mation is both necessary and vital to the tasks an individual is to perform, and many of those called to work in these final hours must be made privy to the inner workings of My Kingdom, and this is given for your protection, knowl- edge, and ability to perform the tasks at hand. The power grid is a place where Heaven and Earth meet and interact; it is not the only place they meet, but it is a very important aspect of the way things function."

The Interaction of God's Light on the Earth

I looked and saw the power grid in place above the Earth, pulsing and undu- lating beautifully, almost as if it had an internal breath. I suddenly saw shafts of light coming down from above—there were thousands upon thousands of multi-colored rainbows and spectrums of light shafts; each intent on specific targets on Earth. As each shaft hit its intended target on Earth, it caused an interaction of light, and the light from the interaction was a result of the response to the shaft of Heaven's light hitting it.

Jesus explained, "The shafts of light are sent from Me—they are the part of Me which I give to My creation to bring them to Myself, and to eternal salvation. Those who accept My gift of light and respond will stay lit, and will then reciprocate and volley their response back up to Me, thus interacting with the power grid. Those who do not accept My light do not stay lit, but quickly go out as soon as the light withdraws. The function is much like a wick that is lit with a burning flame; if the wick does not take the flame and react to the fire it will not, in itself, stay burning once the flame is withdrawn. But if the wick accepts the flame and takes the elements of the light within itself, then it also becomes a little light and a burning flame. The wick represents the spirit of man; each man has a spirit; each spirit has a will; each will has a destiny; each destiny has a place in history."

Jesus continued, "Pray that your wick stays burning and constantly flaming, brighter and higher. Pray that you burn so brightly and highly that you in turn light other dry and wet wicks that so desperately need the light of My living truth."

The Purpose of the Power Grid

Jesus is a wonderful and patient teacher. He teaches me for a while and then, knowing He has given me a lot to ingest, gives me time to absorb it all.

This vision of the power grid continued over several weeks. Some days there was quite a lot to see and learn, and other days it was a time to think about what had already been shown. One day the Lord told me, "This kind of learning lasts. It is not given in one lump sum, but it is given like a multi-course meal, or a class that goes on for weeks." A few days later in prayer, I was in the Spirit and saw the power grid again; and Jesus began to teach: "The power grid is one of the outward expressions of the interaction between Heaven and Earth. Anyone spiritually minded and active can discern being part of the power grid. All celestial beings see it and know of its purpose and function. It is designed both as a spiritual barometer and a testimony to the glory that is even now beginning to cover the Earth, as the waters cover the sea."

....for the earth shall be full of the knowledge of the LORD, as the waters cover the sea. And in that day there shall be a root of Jesse, which shall stand for an ensign of the people; to it shall the Gentiles seek; and his rest shall be glorious. [1]

Prayers Shining Bright

We were back up in the celestial heights watching the power grid once more, but instead of that one shaft of light, and its interaction, I saw the whole Mideast at the present time. There were millions of shafts of light coming up and meeting in the middle, and many interactions from earthly light interacting with the purer and unobstructed heavenly light. My attention was drawn to another place over the Earth, and suddenly we were directly over a group of people praying in Cambodia. These were very young people; most were upper teens and early 20's. I could not understand what they were saying but Jesus was my interpreter and told me they were praying for freedom from oppression, for salvation for their race, and for their brothers and sisters all over the world. They were very earnest and very vocal, with many of the faces wet with tears. Then I saw huge golden shafts of light coming up from this prayer meeting to merge with the power grid, creating a much bigger effect than if just one or two had responded to God. It was like comparing the difference between a small firecracker's light and an atomic bomb, and the repercussions that occurred as this group of people prayed were astronomical! I saw that as the prayers and requests came up, they merged with the power grid and joined with the great responsive fireball lights that were coming down, at great speed, to join their individual lights. As these light forces joined, great light explosions took place. Each joining caused huge ripples of rainbow light to go out and reverberate, not only horizontally over the top of the power grid but also vertically, back down in ripples to the Earth; and as I looked up I saw ripples extending up into the hidden heavens above these massive response lights as well. I saw that the greater the exchange of light, the wider ripples, the more powerful the effect.

Then I observed a group of a few people praying in the United States. None of them were together physically, but they were in contact and were in one accord, praying or declaring the same things. Some of them were separated not just by hundreds but by thousands of miles; yet when their prayers went up and joined with the power grid, it was as if there was no distance at all between them. The same exchange of light occurred, and while it didn't appear at first glance to be as strong as the light ripples from the Cambodian prayer meeting, as it rose and interacted with the light from God's response light above, it became the same power and size as the Cambodian prayer meeting as the individual or small team responses rippled back up to Heaven, merging with the power waves of God's light.

Keys to My Understanding of the Power Grid

Jesus then gave me twenty main keys to understand the power grid. In His words:

1. The main purpose of the power grid is to glorify Me and to show to the world, and all principalities and rulers of all dominions, that I am both Lord and King of all.

2. There are no limits to function by a responsive heart.

3. The only limits to interaction are fear, doubt, unbelief and ignorance.

4. The power grid is for the benefit and use of all believers, but only the believers who respond can actively participate in the power grid and its intended purpose.

5. There is no limit to the amount of light any one person can receive in response to My light.

6. The power grid glorifies Me because it shows the interaction of each person's life as it meets My light, in heaven's rarified, ether air.

7. The power grid acts as a spiritual barometer of spiritual activity all over the earth.

8. One of the main reasons I am teaching you about the power grid is because your life has been a very lonely existence, and you have felt alone and spiritually isolated in your intercession for quite some time.

9.Being aware of the power grid and how it functions will increase your faith: it will help you to know that no one is ever physically alone, unless they want to be; and no one ever needs to feel un-connected, especially to Me, and to others of like mind.

10. The greater the response to the shafts of My light, which are Myself, because I am the Light, the greater each individual's own light becomes.

11. The lesser the response, or lack of it, the lesser My response becomes, although in mercy I will attempt to relight each person's wick if it has gone out or wavered, and I will do this throughout their entire lifetime.

12. The reason the light appears rainbow-colored, and only golden until touched with My light from above, is that the fullness of the spectrums of design, destiny and the interaction of My Spirit, which are varied and represented by the color variations seen in the prism, are symbolic of the fullness of Myself which comes from interaction with a responsive heart.

13. Any believer with a responsive heart can join in at will, any time and without limit, with any others actively responding to Me and functioning on the power grid. They can request to participate in and join in their response, thereby greatly adding to their own individual response. However, it is of key importance to be of one heart and one mind. For instance, if you are praying alone, and are interceding about raising the tide of righteousness in America, you might ask to join in the prayers of all others now actively responding and functioning on power grid.

14. If at any time you are led to intercede for a certain need, area, or country, you can ask Me and I will show you the power grid at that time over that area. Then you will be privy to inside information and can judge the activity, or lack thereof, and be better equipped in prayer.

15. You can also ask Me to show you the shaft of light between the power grid and an individual person. This is helpful to see how much, if any, activity is occurring, and thereby you will be privy to inside information.

16. Each person's response to My light is reciprocated upwards in their individual tunnel shafts, which house and contain their own expressions. As each person's expressions and response volley upwards, their response meets with My light on the power grid, and explosions and wonders take place of an eternal nature.

17. Many that you know to be apostles and founders of the faith have left behind shafts of responsive light, some of which are still burning today. This is illustrated by the scripture, "Not one word will return void, but will accomplish the purpose for which I have sent it." [2] Part of My reason for giving My words in the first place to certain ones who penned the Bible, was to encourage and inspire you in your own connections and responses to Me. Some of these great ones burned so brightly with their responses and declarations, that even though they have passed from death to eternal life, their responses to My light, when they were in their earthly bodies, are still transmitting light and life today.

18. Anyone that is spiritual can enjoy the light still being paraded as a beacon of hope to all who will choose to see.

19. Some will see it by reading the Word itself; but others, among whom you are now included, can look at certain areas of the world where these great ones lived their earthly lives and you can enjoy the light trails they left behind, many of which are still burning brightly.

20. In your present times of intercessory prayer and response, choose to join in the light waves that certain champions of My light have left behind. This is both for your inspiration, encouragement, and example.

The Lord then reminded me of how in the past I have been inspired by many of these 'champion light trails' others have left. Many times after reading a Psalm, or some other scripture, I have been inspired to receive a melody or song, which was directly inspired from the light trails they have left behind.

Seclusion Breeds Intensity

Then I looked, and I was up in the high heavens again, looking down on the glorious power grid. I could see pinpricks of light shafts all over the Earth, rising in response to the rainbow-colored shafts of power and love-light God was sending. Some areas were so concentrated with responsive light shafts that I could not discern the difference of one from another. In other sparsely-populated areas, there were relatively fewer shafts of light coming down to Earth and back up, yet I observed that some of the greatest and most beautiful and powerful shafts of light burning were in some of the most remote places where there were only one or two people. I asked Jesus about this and He explained, "It is because seclusion breeds intensity. Involvement with other people and jobs involving much activity can hinder spiritual connection, activity and growth. This is why many I called to service were, at some point in their lives, imprisoned or secreted away to be alone, so they could concentrate on receiving more of Me and giving in a purer and richer way without as much outside interference."

The lessons about the power grid will no doubt go on, but for now this is what the Lord has shown me regarding it. If you are reading this, my prayer is that His light and the knowledge of the power grid and its function will bring you closer to Him, and you will be able to be used for His Kingdom and its purposes. May we all fulfill the destiny that is written of us in His holy books.

CHAPTER SIX

Introducing the Doors

"I hear you knocking, but you can't come in…" The lyrics echoed in my mind but I (Barbara) couldn't remember the tune, so I Googled it and Wikipedia came through again. Now the tune is stuck in my mind, playing over, and over, and over:

> *I Hear You Knocking* (or *I Hear You Knockin'*) is a rhythm and blues song…It was first recorded by New Orleans rhythm and blues artist Smiley Lewis in 1955. The song tells of the return of a former lover who is rebuffed and features prominent piano accompaniment. *I Hear You Knocking* reached number two in the Billboard R&B singles chart in 1955 and subsequently has been recorded by numerous artists. The original song lyrics are:

> > You went away and left me long time ago
> > Now you're comin' back knockin' on my door
> > I hear you knockin', but you can't come in
> > I hear you knockin', go back where you been[1]

How often do we treat Jesus like the old lover in that song, rejecting His pleas of love, even though He never "went away and left a long time ago"? In reality, He never just walks away,[2] but continually waits for us to let Him into our lives:

Behold, I stand at the door and knock. If anyone hears My voice and opens the door, I will come in to him and dine with him, and he with Me.[3]

I am the door. If anyone enters by Me, he will be saved, and will go in and out and find pasture.[4]

As we've entered into heavenly places, we've learned that there's a lot more to understand about doors than our usual definition. As a noun, a door is a moveable barrier for opening and closing an entranceway; a doorway; a building, house, or the like as represented by its entrance (i.e. two doors up the street); or a means of access (i.e. a door to learning). 'Door' may also be used as idiom such as to 'lay at someone's door' (holding someone accountable), or to 'show someone the door' (order them to leave).[5]

We often visit heavenly places in our dreams; places where God may reveal His truths through visual symbols, and doors are a good example of how everyday objects may hold a variety of meanings in 'dreamspeak'. We've already seen how Jesus relates to a door, so He may be the One to whom a dream about a door points; but the meaning may also relate to our common understanding, with a door representing any of the aspects of its definition (i.e. opportunity, entry, access). Going a bit farther, a description of the door(s) may offer enhanced understanding. For example, we would probably think of a squeaky door as one that needs to be oiled, but in a dream it could indicate a need of the Anointing; a back door may indicate something that is secret or in the past, and a front door the future; going from one door to another could indicate witnessing; and more than one closed door might represent either a choice that needs to be made or some kind of blockage.

In March 2007, Jill Austin prophesied at a conference at Aslan's Place:

Epicenter here, there's this whole region here of the desert. It's a region...a sound. What I keep seeing is the church...and I feel like there's also an apostolic gate at the center. And it's going to be a connecting of wheels within wheels. There will be wheels of a kind of glory train that's on a different highway, a track. And what I keep getting now is cyberspace. You're moving in this realm of doors and spaces, you understand wealth and portals, and you're going to be given language to describe heavenly realms and beings.

And I keep seeing this whole thing of music and sound and movement in this kind of cyberspace, web media, it's like you're positioned here, but it's like wheels within wheels that are moving on this track of this train of this highway of glory... Am I making sense? Oh!!! I just feel like [you must] get ready for the glory of the Lord, and the Lord says that your position is in the discernment—to hold the scrolls that the Lord would have you receive [for] the peoples of God.

To be honest, at the time we had little understanding what this could mean; but in retrospect it is a true account of what has happened, as well as an accurate description of ongoing surprises. Early in 2010, the Lord showed Paul that a very short window of opportunity was open to begin doing ministry via the web. Why short? We didn't know, but the webinar equipment was obtained and a team was trained to operate it. Then, almost immediately, the door slammed shut as the city began doing everything in its power to close down the ministry of Aslan's Place. It certainly seemed as if this train had gone off the track; but no, for God was still at work behind the scenes, and even as the door to ministry seemed to be closing, He was preparing a new one for us to walk through. Early in 2011, He made the way for Aslan's Place to move to a new property where there would be no city interference; a place that is perfectly suited for the changes God would bring and for the move into cyberspace of which Jill spoke. As the journey into the "realm of doors and spaces" escalated, so did the international outreach now possible through the webinars.

The idea for Paul and I to write a book together was also birthed in 2011, and we began writing a few articles that would eventually become chapters, but it seemed like our book train was moving very slowly with a lot of starts and stops. Meanwhile, new revelation began exploding (and continues to explode), and the content of our planned book became so overwhelming that we decided to write *Exploring Heavenly Places* as a series, with various authors contributing in order to share ongoing revelation as it develops. Increased revelation about doors and gates is what came next.

CHAPTER SEVEN

Introducing the Gates

Have you ever been up close and personal with a skunk? Not a good idea!!! My (Barbara's) mother recalled her encounter with one as a girl, playing in a field with her siblings and their dog. Imagine how rambunctious an unrestrained dog can be with several kids urging him on; and this one was joyfully running around, sniffing and digging when he happened upon a skunk's hole. Oh, this was just too good to pass up so he investigated further—pawing away at that tantalizing mystery. I'm sure you can also imagine what happened next as the poor skunk finally had enough and let loose with its aromatic perfume! Mom said her dad was really upset because he had to take all of their clothes out and bury them—there was simply no way they could be salvaged.

I have my own skunk story. Our neighborhood, while well developed, remains home to a large variety of animals that are drawn to the brushy hillsides and nearby creek. When we moved here, we put a wrought iron fence around our front patio and made sure the bars on the bottom were very close together to keep our little dog in and the rabbits out. One day our neighbor was out walking her dog at dawn and, passing our gate, noticed a skunk on our patio that seemed to be looking unsuccessfully for a way out. An old ranch-hand who'd dealt with many such critters over the years, she wasn't intimidated and—luckily for us—knew exactly what to do. She moved over to a spot where she could not be seen and made enough noise to distract the skunk, causing him to move away from the gate. Then she quietly opened it and moved out of sight. Within a few moments a very calm skunk ambled out onto the sidewalk and scurried off into the bushes. Had my husband hurried out the door on his way to work and surprised our little visitor, we may have had to dig a hole somewhere for his clothes too! We definitely learned the importance of a secure gate with no gaps for unwelcome visitors to squeeze through. It was just a tiny gap—only about an inch more than the rest of the fence, but it was enough. Needless to say, that gap has been closed and the gate secured.

The Bible has a lot to say about gates: whether they are open or closed, as well as what occurs in them. It's a subject most of us have probably not considered in years gone by, focusing instead on the heavier theological issues of sin, judgment, Heaven and Hell, forgiveness, grace, love, redemption, mercy, etc.; or just enjoying the wonderful stories of biblical heroes such as Noah, Moses, Esther, David, Jesus and His disciples. But since everything the Bible says has tremendous value, let's explore the more obscure topic of gates.

One summer, as a child attending Vacation Bible School, I recall vividly the scripture that was used each morning as the call to worship:

> *Lift up your heads, O you gates! And be lifted up, you everlasting doors! And the King of glory shall come in. Who is this King of glory? The LORD strong and mighty, the LORD mighty in battle. Lift up your heads, O you gates! Lift up, you everlasting doors! And the King of glory shall come in. Who is this King of glory? The LORD of hosts, He is the King of glory.*[1]

I also remember wondering what in the world that meant. How could gates have heads? It sounded good as everyone recited the verses out loud, but it made absolutely no sense to my young mind. However, the implications of this verse are profound, and we will gain a clearer understanding of its meaning as we continue.

Both gates and doors provide the security for enclosed spaces—if open, entry is possible; if closed and/or locked, the interior spaces are secured from intrusion. Logically though, there is a slight difference between gates and doors, as gates generally lead into larger spaces and doors into smaller ones. For example, there may be a gate into a yard through which one must enter before reaching a door into a home or building. On a bigger scale, we can visualize the oft-visited gates around Buckingham Palace or the Vatican, the gates of an amusement park, or the gates of a city (i.e. Jerusalem)—all designed to provide or block entry. On the other end of the spectrum, there are tiny, microscopic gates on the cells in our bodies, which are defined as molecules, or parts of molecules, that act in response to a stimulus to permit or block passage through a cell membrane.[2] Consider just one cell in the body and realize that within it there are thousands of parts, including the chromosomes, which are composed of DNA—God's blueprint for the entire body. Certainly, if viewed this way, even a tiny cell gate could be considered an entrance into a much greater dimensional space—entire volumes are written about cellular biology, which is something we can't even observe without a microscope.

As we cannot easily see microscopic gates, neither is it an easy thing to observe gates that exist in the unseen spiritual realms; but that doesn't make them any less real. This is evident in scripture by references to the gates of Sheol, death, and Hades or to the gates of righteousness, Heaven, the Lord, and the City of God.[3] And, like the physical examples of cells or cities, spiritual gates also seem to enter into dimensions while spiritual doors enter into smaller places such as rooms or chambers.

The gate of a city, as described in the Bible, was often a fortified structure that was deeper than the wall.

> All these cities were fortified with high walls, gates, and bars, besides a great many rural towns.[4]

Nehemiah 2:7-8 reveals that within major cities there were usually strongly fortified citadels with gates:

> Furthermore I said to the king, "If it pleases the king, let…a letter [be given] to Asaph the keeper of the king's forest, that he must give me timber to make beams for the gates of the citadel which pertains to the temple, for the city wall, and for the house that I will occupy. [5]

Yet, we also see that certain gates were only the thickness of a curtain:

> And for the gate of the court [of the tabernacle] shall be an hanging of twenty cubits…The screen for the gate of the court was woven of blue, purple, and scarlet

thread, and of fine woven linen. The length was twenty cubits, and the height along its width was five cubits, corresponding to the hangings of the court.[6]

We know from Luke 23:45 that the curtain into the Holy of Holies was torn in two at the crucifixion. So here's a thought to ponder—as the curtain was described as a physical gate, and as the physical reality is a representation or shadow of the spiritual reality, perhaps we can conclude that the physical rending of the curtain was a visual manifestation of the destruction of a gate that was erected to keep mankind from God after Adam and Eve sinned. Recall the words of Genesis 3:24:

> *So He drove out the man; and He placed cherubim at the east of the garden of Eden, and a flaming sword which turned every way, to guard the way to the tree of life.*

So, at the instant that the barrier gate was destroyed by Jesus' atoning sacrifice, a new gate was opened—a gate of righteousness, a gate of redemption, a gate through which all people who choose Jesus may enter.

It appears obvious that, as in all things He created, God's original intent was for gates to be good. Unfortunately, the righteous purposes for which they were designed are often corrupted by evil, as ungodly men demand their own ways. The ongoing struggle of good versus evil that is so evident today, was evidenced thousands of years ago, when the godly King Josiah:

> *Brought all the priests from the cities of Judah, and defiled the high places where the priests had burned incense, from Geba to Beersheba; also he broke down the high places at the gates which were at the entrance of the Gate of Joshua the governor of the city, which were to the left of the city gate.*[7]

Then, as now, those determined not to follow God continued upon their evil path:

> *Nevertheless, the priests of the high places did not come up to the altar of the LORD in Jerusalem, but they ate unleavened bread among their brethren.*[8]

Like Josiah, we have a mandate regarding gates:

> *Enter into His gates with thanksgiving, and into His courts with praise.*[9]

Blessed is the man who listens to me, watching daily at my gates, waiting at the posts of my doors.[10]

Hate evil, love good; establish justice in the gate.[11]

These are the things you shall do: speak each man the truth to his neighbor; give judgment in your gates for truth, justice, and peace.[12]

Enter by the narrow gate; for wide is the gate and broad is the way that leads to destruction, and there are many who go in by it. Because narrow is the gate and difficult is the way which leads to life, and there are few who find it.[13]

Do not rob the poor because he is poor, nor oppress the afflicted at the gate; for the Lord will plead their cause, and plunder the soul of those who plunder them.[14]

We are also instructed to enter into covenant, peace, and the joy of the Lord,[15] all of which are likely examples of the gates of righteousness.

We must take note of the truth that we are called to choose the narrow gate—the difficult path. How sad that we live in a society that is so pleasure-oriented that we are conditioned to look for short cuts and easy answers. How sad that many of us are so focused on our rights and/or entitlements that if we look honestly at our lives, we might be surprised to see that we are on a broad way. Individually and corporately, as the church of the Living God, we must wake up to our responsibilities at the gates—we must make the righteous choices. Otherwise, we may soon find ourselves identifying too closely with the sorrowful lament over Jerusalem:

Her gates have sunk into the ground; He has destroyed and broken her bars. Her king and her princes are among the nations; the Law is no more, and her prophets find no vision from the LORD.[16]

Instead, we can look to Jesus as our example, for He made the tough decisions so we can be free. Rather than seeking sanctuary inside the gates of Heaven:

Therefore Jesus also, that He might sanctify the people with His own blood, suffered outside the gate.[17]

Aside from the fact that He suffered for us, why is it so significant that it occurred outside the gate? Probably many reasons, but for our purposes, consider two. First, sin is so detestable to God that when a priest would make a sin offering, it was done outside the camp. Second, people who were required to live outside the gate were those considered to be unclean, such as the lepers. Without Jesus' outside-the-gate sacrifice when He became sin for us, we would eternally be unclean, and unfit to enter into the gates of Heaven ourselves.

Everything that exists around the throne of God is alive. Today, those who are caught up into the heavens in much the same way as Ezekiel, the Apostle Paul or John the Revelator were, frequently report that everything they see is living. So it only makes sense that gates of righteousness, like everything else originally created by God, are infused with life. More than once, gates are personified in scripture:

> *Her gates shall lament and mourn.*[18]

> *Wail. O gate! Cry, O city!*[19]

> *Judah mourns, and her gates languish; they mourn for the land, and the cry of Jerusalem has gone up.*[20]

Psalm 24:7-10 now begins to make a lot more sense to me than it did as a child in Vacation Bible School, and I often notice that my spirit is crying out:

> *Lift up your heads, O you gates! And be lifted up, you everlasting doors! And the King of glory shall come in. Who is this King of glory? The LORD strong and mighty, the LORD mighty in battle. Lift up your heads, O you gates! Lift up, you everlasting doors! And the King of glory shall come in.*

> *Who is this King of glory? The LORD of hosts, He is the King of glory.*[21]

CHAPTER EIGHT

Earthly and Heavenly Gates

Throughout scripture, whether a reference is to the earthly or heavenly version of the city of Jerusalem, it is clear that it is near and dear to God's heart. Both are gated, and an entire book could be written about the spiritual significance of this. For example, Jesus referred to himself as the gate of the sheep,[1] and Ezekiel prophesied His use of the Eastern Gate.[2] Scriptural references to the physical gates of Jerusalem abound, with the most comprehensive information being found in Nehemiah. Even so, the exact location of walls and gates of biblical Jerusalem are often in doubt due to the lack of strong archeological and historical evidence,[3] and it appears that different names are used for the same gates in various historical and biblical writings. References to the city gates include:[4] Sheep Gate;[5] Fish Gate;[6] Old Gate;[7] Valley Gate;[8] Dung Gate,[9] which is probably the same as Harsith Gate and sometimes rendered the Gate of Potsherds;[10] Fountain Gate;[11] Water Gate;[12] Horse Gate;[13] East Gate;[14] Miphkad Gate, or Inspection Gate;[15] Ephraim Gate;[16] Prison Gate, or Gate of the Guard;[17] Corner Gate;[18] Benjamin Gate;[19] First Gate;[20] Joshua Gate;[21] Foundation Gate.[22]

Ezekiel 48:31-35 is prophetic of the twelve gates of the heavenly Jerusalem, each of which are named for a tribe of Israel:

The gates of the city shall be named after the tribes of Israel, the three gates northward: one gate for Reuben, one gate for Judah, and one gate for Levi; on the east side, four thousand five hundred cubits, three gates: one gate for Joseph, one gate for Benjamin, and one gate for Dan; on the south side, measuring four thousand five hundred cubits, three gates: one gate for Simeon, one gate for Issachar, and one gate for Zebulun; on the west side, four thousand five hundred cubits with their three gates: one gate for Gad, one gate for Asher, and one gate for Naphtali.

Revelation 21 not only confirms Ezekiel account, but also adds some wonderful details:

- The city has a great and high wall with twelve angels at the gates.
- The names of the twelve tribes of the children of Israel are written on them.
- The twelve gates are twelve pearls, with each individual gate being one pearl.
- The gates shall not be shut by day, and there shall be no night there.
- Those who follow His commandments will be given the right to the tree of life, and may enter through the gates into the city.

Crystal Kain Ross experienced an encounter with the Lord as He showed her three of the gates into His heavenly City of Light. When another trusted intercessor/seer read her account she was astounded because it revealed exactly what she had also been shown, reporting that as she read she would think, "Well, surely she's not going to say this, or that." But sure enough, the very next sentence would mirror her own experience.

Crystal's vision:

As I looked left and then right, I saw that we were standing near the middle of the east side. I observed three massive gates, each spaced a great distance apart. I wondered just how far apart they were, and Jesus responded to my unspoken question aloud saying, "Almost 500 Earth miles between them."

Before me was the most amazing sight I have ever beheld—above me, so high that its top disappeared into celestial pink and cream heavenly clouds, was a gate made up of a single pearl. This was not a gate comprised of pearls that were crushed up or laid together in some pattern to make a gate this massive—no! It was a solid, single pearl making up this one gate. I wondered if the other gates were made of single pearls and as I looked to Jesus for the answer, He replied again to my unspoken question, "Yes!"

I stood there looking up. My vision had been supernaturally enhanced so that not only could I see down the entire length of the wall from left to right, but also I could see all the way up to the top of the wall—the entirety of the massive gate made from a single pearl.

The waves of light emanating out from within the pearly gate were tangible—a little like seeing the faint lines of a mirage shimmering over the road on a hot summer day.

This gate had a round seal upon which was written in etchings of glowing light, "The Gate of Judah". The seal was situated on the middle of the pearl, taking up a quarter of its width, and underneath the name, the inscription continued "…of the City of Light." There was also an etching of an almost imperceptible figure of a lion with three small cubs at its feet at the base of a rock. The lion was facing toward the right, with its left paw up on the rock and its right paw overshadowing the three cubs. It was looking in the direction in which the gate opened (from right to left). The mane of the lion seemed especially beautiful, with waved etchings that glowed and almost seemed to lift off the pearl, like love waves blowing in the gentle, celestial wind. The lion seemed to be getting ready to let out a full roar with his mouth wide open.

I glanced over at Jesus. He was smiling. He seemed to enjoy watching me discover all the details of the majestic beauty of the City of His Light as much as I did. He broke into my thoughts asking, "Do you know why I brought you to this gate first?"

I answered, "No, why?"

Jesus replied, "It is because everyone I have created belongs to one of these tribes symbolically, even Adam and Eve. Everyone that comes to Our City of Light will enter through the individual gate to which they symbolically belong."

This was an interesting thought to me, because for years I have felt a special kinship to the tribe of Judah. One of the verses I really like that talks about Judah is, "Send Judah first and the battle will be won."

Then Jesus interrupted my thoughts again with this statement, "You are attached to the tribe of Judah spiritually, and it is this very gate to which you shall come when you come home to stay."

Another surprising detail was that the color of the pearl was not stark heavenly white or cream, but was golden gossamer amber, much like the color of a lion shining in the sun. It was not a solid golden color, but was like golden amber swirled with the mix of angel's wings and celestial clouds. In a word, astonishing!

Jesus asked me if I would like to see the two other gates and I enthusiastically responded, "Yes! Let's go!"

He took me to the gate on our right. It was exactly the same size as the Gate of Judah but the color was slightly different. On this gate was inscribed, "The Gate of Issachar," and below that inscription, as on the Gate of Judah, it read, "…of the City of Light." The color of the pearl was a very soft opalescent pearl/gray of the lightest shade, with the same swirling gossamer angelic wing pattern interspersed. The swirling pattern made it look as if it had been polished in millions of round swirls until it shone and glowed. The etched figure to the right of the name crest was a donkey standing with full packs on both sides. It was facing to the right, like lion had been, but was standing on level ground.

Then Jesus took me back past the Gate of Judah and over to another gate, which was labeled, "The Gate of Zebulun." It was just like the other two, but the color of this pearl was tinted the tiniest, slightest, breathy color of azure blue; more like breath and wind than color. It was like looking at the color of the bluest sky on the brightest day. Like the others, it had the unmistakable swirls of angel wings and celestial clouds within the color of the pearl. The symbol to the right of the name crest was a large ship with a single mast and sail. The sail appeared as if it had breath in it, and was facing towards the east in the same direction as the other gate symbols. The ship was sitting in the middle of a sea with mighty waves, and it was perched in a slanted fashion near the crest of the wave, as if having total mastery of it.

All of the gates were very beautiful, but I was partial to the Gate of Judah. The lion appeared very protective of the three little cubs, and the color of it was like the burnished gold that decorates much in those realms—royal and lovely. As Jesus and I began walking, we supernaturally ended up back at the Gate of Judah in just a few minutes.

Certainly, the wonder of the heavenly gates will astound us! But lest we forget, it is worth remembering that there are also spiritual gates through which we do not want to pass:

And I also say to you that you are Peter, and on this rock I will build My church, and the gates of Hades shall not prevail against it.[23]

Where then is my hope? As for my hope, who can see it? Will they go down to the gates of Sheol? Shall we have rest together in the dust?[24]

CHAPTER NINE
Legal Significance of Gates

There is much legal significance attached to the concept of gates. Biblically, the gates of the city were where the elders met to conduct official business, as well as the location of the courts and the execution of justice.

> *You shall appoint judges and officers in all your gates, which the LORD your God gives you, according to your tribes, and they shall judge the people with just judgment.*[1]

> *Then his father and his mother shall take hold of him and bring him out to the elders of his city, to the gate of his city.*[2]

> *Now Boaz went up to the gate and sat down there; and behold, the close relative of whom Boaz had spoken came by. So Boaz said, "Come aside, friend, sit down here." So he came aside and sat down.*[3]

It is also evident that if a public statement was to be made in a way that sent a very clear message, gates were a good place to do it. Consider the warnings and/or prophetic implications of these verses:

> *And the king of Ai he hanged on a tree until evening. And as soon as the*

sun was down, Joshua commanded that they should take his corpse down from the tree, cast it at the entrance of the gate of the city, and raise over it a great heap of stones that remains to this day.[4]

Then it happened, when he made mention of the ark of God, that Eli fell off the seat backward by the side of the gate; and his neck was broken and he died, for the man was old and heavy. And he had judged Israel forty years.[5]

Then the five men who had gone to spy out the land went up. Entering there, they took the carved image, the ephod, the household idols, and the molded image. The priest stood at the entrance of the gate with the six hundred men who were armed with weapons of war.[6]

Then Joshua charged them at that time, saying, "Cursed be the man before the LORD who rises up and builds this city Jericho; he shall lay its foundation with his firstborn, and with his youngest he shall set up its gates... In his days Hiel of Bethel built Jericho. He laid its foundation with Abiram his firstborn, and with his youngest son Segub he set up its gates, according to the word of the LORD, which He had spoken through Joshua the son of Nun.[7]

Gates are strategic in regard to the security of those within their walls—if one dwells within a gate there is a presumption of safety:

And the Levite, because he has no portion nor inheritance with you, and the stranger and the fatherless and the widow who are within your gates, may come and eat and be satisfied, that the LORD your God may bless you in all the work of your hand which you do.[8]

If there is among you a poor man of your brethren, within any of the gates in your land which the LORD your God is giving you, you shall not harden your heart nor shut your hand from your poor brother.[9]

Gather the people together, men and women and little ones, and the stranger who is within your gates, that they may hear and that they may learn to fear the LORD your God and carefully observe all the words of this law.[10]

You shall not give back to his master the slave who has escaped from his master to you. He may dwell with you in your midst, in the place which he chooses within one of your gates, where it seems best to him; you shall not oppress him.[11]

You shall not oppress a hired servant who is poor and needy, whether one of your brethren or one of the aliens who is in your land within your gates.[12]

Given the security that is implied by gates, it is not surprising that they are the point at which an enemy seeks to penetrate one's defenses:

They shall besiege you at all your gates until your high and fortified walls, in which you trust, come down throughout all your land; and they shall besiege you at all your gates throughout all your land which the LORD your God has given you.[13]

When the Gazites were told, "Samson has come here!" they surrounded the place and lay in wait for him all night at the gate of the city. They were quiet all night, saying, "In the morning, when it is daylight, we will kill him.[14]

One evening in January 2011, when Paul and Donna Cox, my husband and I (Barbara) were praying for Donna because she was about to have surgery, Paul discerned a gate. As he explored it, he determined that there were really two gates with one opening in each direction—one in and one out—and he thought it might have to do with past and future events. Doing further research the next day, I was led to information regarding Janus, the Roman god of gates for whom January is named. Interestingly, he is most often depicted as having two heads facing opposite directions; one head looks back at the last year while the other looks forward to the year ahead, so that he is simultaneously looking into the future and the past.[15]

Paul also discerned that there were such gates in front of each of us. We began asking the Lord what this could mean, and it was revealed that they were unrighteous gates that had been opened by gossip that had been spoken against us. As we sought to understand this more clearly, it became evident that three of the four of us had gates opened by a specific individual while one did not, and that all of us had gates that had been opened by a second individual.[16] Proof positive it seems, that we must diligently guard our speech, heeding the admonition of James 3:5-6:

Even so the tongue is a little member and boasts great things. See how great a forest a little fire kindles! And the tongue is a fire, a world of iniquity. The tongue is so set among our members that it defiles the whole body, and sets on fire the course of nature; and it is set on fire by hell.

I'm certain that we have very little comprehension of the power of our spoken words to effect the opening and/or closing of spiritual gates—gates of righteousness as well as those of unrighteousness. Perhaps unrighteousness is able to come and go in generational lines via ungodly gates that have been empowered by sin. If that is the case, let us determine always to speak blessings rather than curses.

CHAPTER TEN

Open and Closed Gates and Doors

As the new revelation regarding gates and doors began, Paul and his intercessors started discerning them around the people for whom they were praying during ministry sessions. One young man was seeing gates on every cell, even though he was unaware of the biological truth of his vision.

Following the admonition of Hebrews 5:14 to train our senses, Paul began practicing whenever gates manifested in a prayer session, not really knowing what he was doing at the time, but following the Lord's direction by faith. It wasn't long before he was in a meeting in Ontario, Canada with a friend who was suffering terribly with Crohn's disease. At the time, we were doing mostly generational prayer and many of us had prayed everything we knew to pray, but nothing seemed to work. In fact, our friend was becoming steadily worse. But on that day, the power of God suddenly manifested in the room and all of us were literally on the ground, unable to stand before Him. Paul leaned over toward our friend and prayed, "Lord, close these doors," and he was immediately healed. The prayer was very simple and went something like this, "Lord, please open all doors that should be open, and close all doors that should be closed." Everyone was amazed and excited at the miraculous healing, and Paul was thinking, "Maybe we're onto something here."

Soon thereafter, Paul began feeling the grid on his body. He said, "It felt very strange—like a zzzzzzz on my body. I felt bad, so I asked the Lord to clean off these lines, not knowing at the time what I was doing. But there was a spot on my skin that I felt was bad, so I asked Him to clean off the doors. The spot is now gone. I also had a problem with a knuckle that was arthritic, so I prayed the same prayer and my knuckle was healed and there is no more pain."

We believe that a gate is an entrance to a dimension, and within a dimension are many doors. If you picture a hotel corridor there are doors on either side, which is often the way that Paul feels them. Some of our spiritual doors are open but they're not supposed to be, allowing access to the enemy. But at the same time, some doors are closed that should not be closed because they are the access points to blessings.

Certainly we all want the Lord to enter our gates:

> *Lift up your heads, O you gates! And be lifted up, you everlasting doors! And the King of glory shall come in.*[1]

However, it took us a long time to figure some things out, partly because we didn't notice there are differing translations in popular versions of the Bible of the original language for doors and gates. Two very significant scriptures where gates are mentioned appear below in two translations, the NKJV and the ESV. In this case, the correct translation of doors and gates from the original language is found in the ESV. Finally, everything started falling into place and we were able to pair together all that we were discerning with scripture once we realized that the key is the doors, and the doors must be opened in order for the gates to remain open. Compare and contrast the NKJV versus the ESV in the following verses. The significant words are <u>underlined</u> for clarity:

> (NKJV) *Thus says the Lord to His anointed, to Cyrus, whose right hand I have held—to subdue nations before Him and loose the armor of kings, to open before Him the double doors, so that the gates will not be shut: "I will go before you and make the crooked places straight; I will break in pieces the <u>gates of bronze</u> and cut the bars of iron"* [2] *...For He has broken the <u>gates of bronze,</u> and cut the bars of iron in two.*[3]

(ESV) Thus says the Lord to his anointed, to Cyrus, whose right hand I have grasped, to subdue nations before him and to loose the belts of kings, to open doors before him that gates may not be closed: "I will go before you and level the exalted places, I will break in pieces the <u>doors of bronze</u> and cut through the bars of iron" [4] *...For he shatters the <u>doors of bronze</u> and cuts in two the bars of iron.* [5]

Once again, the correct translation of doors and gates from the original language is *<u>doors of bronze</u>*—**not** *<u>gates of bronze</u>*. Now, we often ask the Lord to open and close doors when praying for someone. We also may add a request that He break in pieces all doors of bronze, destroy all bars of iron, and occupy the gates. Sometimes the results are measurable—even dramatic. Other times we observe no changes. Why? We don't know, so we persevere in faith.

As I (Barbara) have prayed with people in this manner, some have reported that they can see doors opening and closing in the spiritual realm—sometimes hundreds of them—and they also see gates being opened wide. In one instance, I asked the Lord to show a lady what He had done and she was astounded by a vision of herself standing on dry ground at the bottom of a dam, similar in size to Hoover Dam. As the floodgates opened, she was engulfed in a rush of water with a current so strong it should have swept her away, but she was able to stand strong in the midst of it. She immediately understood this to be an indication of the powerful cleansing by the Spirit that she had just received.

CHAPTER ELEVEN

The Revelation Continues

As is usual when the Lord begins teaching a new thing, the prophetic words/ insights have continued to unfold over the years. Often, the words come as an angel shows up at a meeting with a message.

February 2, 2011, Angelic Message Received by Jana Green:

> I have entrusted you with much more; had you known you would not have done the things you have done. It is about the remnant crossing the second death. You are being acclimated for position. A heavenly endowment, a requisition; it is about supernatural provision. The heavenly treasure; hook your eye into that. Provision without measure. Eternity holds the key, the key of David. Intimacy. How do you believe for heavenly things when you do not even see what is naturally given? Set your eyes on things above, where your treasure is. There is much more than you ever hoped for or imagined. I am breaking through the veil between Heaven and Earth. You are creating new pathways, pathways of thinking. They are more than neural pathways; eternal perception is where your heart shall be. Believing is seeing and trusting in Me. Gates are access points, places of crossroads. Many have been waylaid from position and purpose and birth-

right. But it is redeemed at the gates both forwards and backwards. Create a new realm and you will remove the markers, the memorials that have been set up on the soul that hold a frequency to cause a loop to return. Memorials. That is why the legion was among the tomb. The memories held him there. Memorials set up by negativity. That is the land of the soul that has not been fully taken. The gates hold the answer and the question. Ask for the access and get the treasure.

June 18, 2011, Angelic Message Received by Jana Green:

Keep shifting. Keep moving. It is the holy way. When you step into the gates you open the expanse. It is wider still for a greater advance. It is a step of faith. It opens up the realms. You must learn and experience the way of the width and expanse. Many will trust, and many maneuver and create from this realm the stewardship of the creator God; it is given to man. I want to release the anointing of greater works. You trust in Me, trust also in the works that I do. So your mind is expanded. Your imagination will ring true. Sanctified to the holy words by the sounds of the creator Yah. Shifting, going in and out; the mystery is hard to explain. Stay where you are, but I move you for the Kingdom in the realm. You have been set aside like a holy abandonment. Not that you are orphans, but I have tested the heart to seek My face, to seek the face of the Holy One, to reveal the mystery of the God of Daniel who is his judge. Practice. Learn in this way. Experience. It is a platform of justice that you may agree; change in Heaven and Earth that you may agree. Build on what you learn for the acceleration of wisdom. I am pouring out My Spirit on all flesh. The divine remnant is to know the mystery through Heaven and Earth, the supernatural creative mystery of the true witness of Yah. For the true sons are in the Earth, the revealed ones.

June 2011, Paul Cox in Miami, Florida:

We started on something about the left ear gate and the thumb and toe, and this is what I saw and heard: a silver-looking container in the shape of a rectangle, catching mud/sludge coming out of the ears or being put into the ears. I then saw some kind of armor-looking thing on my left shoulder and tremendous pain began to be felt there. Several people came up to me and shared that they had the same pain in the left shoulder. As I went to dinner after that, I asked the Lord what this was about. He said, "Completely ready for this revelation." I then asked Him to share what I was ready to hear. He said, "Faith comes by hearing and hearing by the word of God, both the written and spoken word. My children are not listening to either one and this is a result of it." I believe that the armor is tied to the left ear gate, and on the left shoulder is a star gate, for the gates are different.

July 12, 2011, Angelic Message Received by Jana Green:

You have transitioned to the place of change. Authority is in the gates. It has all been arranged. Learn what it means to possess the gates. The key is for the strategies, for the battle is in the gates. Your perception has positioned you to know your place. Identity is of the essence, the gate of grace. You all uniquely have keys building one upon another to set the captives free. From here you go up, from here you go down, height, length and width. Listen to the sound. This is the time of acclamation. Your senses are being renewed. Not just the physical but in the spiritual too. You connect on the right wavelength. It is about position. Learn to possess the gates. Stand your ground. Declare a thing and release the sound.

May 21, 2011, from Jana Green:

For the last couple of days I have been in intercession and trying to birth something in the spiritual realm. I was pushing up against 4 corners, and felt they were gates. I don't think it is one kind of spirit, but a system affecting the people. Sound frequencies seem to increase, as well as vibration, and I think the vibration is coming by way of a gate. I believe it affects every issue that plagues the individual, and a memorial is set up on the soul and/or spirit, like a transducer (an electrical device that converts one form of energy into another). It's like turning sound into sight, which in turn affects the whole person. The gates are the openings that start or stop transference on its path, or where the paths meet. It can cause a recurring pathway for good or evil. Entities stand guard at these gates and doors depending on the created pathway. On the other hand, I have been discerning something good waiting. I believe it is sound wisdom, who cries out where the paths meet, by the way at the gate (Proverbs 8). She is a living power. I would like to tell you more but I am still discovering wisdom and the need to know her.

January 31, 2012, from Persis Tiner:

Doors and keys
And keys and doors
Both intertwined
Both to bring more
To those I adore

Doors and doors and doors and doors
Waiting, waiting
Pulsing, pulsing
The time has come to be explored

Explored by My servant (Paul)
Prepared by My hand   (Paul has been prepared by Him for this)
To bring revelation and knowledge
Throughout the land

Keys
Big and small
Some bright and some dull
Waiting for My servant
To discover the ones
Which will unlock secrets
Which will set captives free
In their search and desperation
Seeking for Me

The year of government
To be found in these doors
Unlocking secrets
To be found in these keys
Many have pieces to help figure out
Just what these doors and keys
Are all about

They hold many weapons
To counter the attacks
Satan and his army
Have planned with great glee
To bring devastation to My people and Me

But wake up the army
Put them on alert
Be not distracted from the work of My word
Ponder it, search it, and think it anew
For it holds much knowledge
And power for you

February 21, 2012, from Jana Green:

It is a whole other dominion level. This is the first of many assignments. The first is the worst; assignment after assignment; victory after victory. You are taking the realms back. Dominion and rule, gate to gate, when wisdom cries out there is no escape. The captives will be redeemed, they will not be denied. It is My heart for My inheritance to thrive. You are positioned correctly. You are positioned for power, for authorized rule. The Kingdom is ours. Smokescreen. It released confusion and depression. Breakthrough. Watch what I do. Each person holds a gate and the gates are possessed. Wisdom is at the gates. You are interrupting the enemy.

March 22, 2012, Persis Tiner regarding Dimension/Realms/Kingdom:

There are kingdoms in the dimensions
The realms and the spheres
Kingdoms locked away
Behind fences and walls
Keeping My people
Unable to fulfill their call

Kingdoms of fear
Of delusions and pain
Kingdoms of little faith
Of no hope in My name

Kingdoms of hopelessness
Despair and torment
Confusion and delusions
Running hand and hand
Behind walls of cement

Who will it be
To bring freedom and sight
To these hopeless and forgotten
These peoples I love
Who will bring freedom
From all of the above?

Come, get out of your boxes
Come into the Light
Exploring new revelation
Embracing the truth
That through Me and by Me
We can win the race

New doors must be open
The media to expose
The lies of the enemy
The falseness he represents
The futility of his promises
Must be exposed

Keep flying
Keep going
Keep opening doors
Keep pulling down walls
And fences galore

Be bold and step out
Of your boxes so safe
Come, jump and jump high
I will catch you for sure
And flying we will go
To dimensions and kingdoms

Yet to unfold

August 12, 2012, Angelic Message Received by Jana Green:

At the gate you divide
Make a discussion
Come decide
Unify the heart to fear His name
This one stands here to proclaim
Heaven and Earth become one
When the heart and the mind are unified, it's divine
From the sound of Heaven the deed will be done
Who stands at the crossroads?
Who stands at the gate?
Is it the janitor of survival or the One who leads to escape?
Be careful what you listen to
Does it bring life?
By wisdom and understanding, that is how you decide
Send the thief away
Possess the gate
From the heart flows the river of life, it's not too late!

An email from Paul Cox on March 15, 2014, sums up our astonishment at the Lord's revelation:

Rob and I have just come to Hong Kong, and we watched movies on the way.

In *Ender's Game,* the theme is releasing children to war with the enemies at the gate! See Psalm 127:5. In Disney's *Frozen,* we see the theme of doors and a gate. The key is to release love so the gate is no longer closed! In one song there is this line, "…and fractals everywhere."

You cannot make this stuff up!

CHAPTER TWELVE
Practicing Discernment

Paul regularly conducts Biblical Discernment and Exploration workshops at Aslan's Place, and many of the sessions are available to view online (also includes transcriptions). All of the information in this chapter and the next, some of which is review, is from such meetings and can be understood in even greater depth by watching the actual sessions,[1] because it can be a little hard to follow in the written format. In an exploration session such as this one, the comments from individuals may or may not clearly relate to the previous statement when transcribed into text, since each is waiting for his or her turn to speak about what they discern. Also, please keep in mind that since this is a forum for learning, not all input will be 100% accurate, but each individual statement is assessed and, like puzzle pieces, come together to form a clear picture by the time all has been said and done.

On January 11, 2014, Paul discerned that a spiritual gate had manifested in the room. At this point he had no further information about what the gate looked like, why it was there or what the group was supposed to do about it. Following is a very condensed step-by-step version of what it looks like to practice discernment in a group setting over the course of about two hours.

• Paul stands up and discerns the gate, demonstrating how he feels it on his body.

• Participants get up and practice discerning, ask questions and give feedback about what they are feeling.

• Paul realizes something is written on the top of the gate from right to left. It is apostolic and it is locked.

• A participant sees the gate and says, "It looks like it's wood. It could be iron but it looks weathered at the top part. Yeah, it's very weathered, like peeling. It's an ungodly declaration on the top of it."

• Paul shows a copy of a previously submitted prophetic word that was written from right to left in tongues. He explains, "I found out that in the Pentecostal movement, which started in 1907 I think, people did this but it was declared to be evil so they stopped them from doing it. I'll tell you, you can feel the anointing (on the submitted word). That's why discernment is so important. As you see, without discernment we embrace some supernatural things that are not of God, yet we do not embrace other things that are of God because they seem so strange. How do you tell the difference? You tell the difference through discernment. Not just by my discernment. It's by our discernment together. You see, it's together, and if some of you said, 'I don't know about this,' then I would stop because that would be an indication to me that perhaps this is not of God. But you see, no one person can determine if something is truly of God. That's a big mistake we're making in the church today—regarding the one person in the front we say, 'Yeah, they are a prophet of God,' and that's very possibly true. But you know what? We need each other. That is what the church is. There's only one head—it's Christ—and the rest of us are trying to find our way together. But we need to do it together. That's why we sit like this in a circle, because we're all equal."

• Participant offers a picture on her cell phone that she thinks look like the gate, which is then projected onto a big screen for all to see.

• Participant who offered the written word draws a picture of how he sees the gate.

• Paul selects a participant who is a seer to stand at the gate and try to read the script, and she says, "He who has an ear, let him hear what the Spirit of the Lord has to say" (reading the writing on the screen from right to left). The gate is a key. And I came to this understanding because 7 has sort of been a predominant thing and I just see a 7. That's the way that you write 7 in Europe with the line across.

• Paul responds, "When she did that, did you feel the anointing? It says in 1 Corinthians 14 that we should judge the Word, so we're judging you, but not in a bad way; it means to evaluate."

• Participant says, "I just want to share that when you had us come and feel it I was feeling the letter saying 'Heaven.' And I asked myself, 'Am I hearing a right thing?' Then right away, 'It's a fake.'" Paul responds, "a fake?" Participant confirms, "a fake."

• Paul says, "There's something about evangelism with this. Evangelism, prophetic—in fact it may even be the fivefold—apostolic, evangelism, prophetic, pastor, teacher."

• Participant says, "What we're doing here is the apostolic model," and Paul agrees.

• Paul continues, "Now what is the everlasting curse? People say there are ones that go down through the 3rd and 4th generation, but there are also everlasting curses. David was told that the sword would never leave his house. That's an everlasting curse. Samuel was told that because of the actions of his sons, Hophni and Phinehas, there would never be an old man in his house, which is an everlasting curse of premature death."

• Participant refers to the comment about 'Heaven' and says, "I saw it was like a counterfeit gate to Heaven; you know, like the pearly gates, and you think it's for people to enter into Heaven. But this is not to enter Heaven; this for those that come for other reasons—maybe it's religion—and they are coming to what they think is Heaven."

• Paul says, "Right! OK, let's go to Isaiah 45." And Paul proceeds to teach about gates and doors to give background to the group.

• Participant says, "I saw a gate and then a door. It's like a metal gate and then the door, but not the door you are touching."

• Paul gets up to discern what is happening and feels an ungodly power standing in front of one door, as well as an apostolic watcher and an apostolic power at a second door. Then he goes back to discern what is inside the two doors. He feels a lot of evil coming out of the first door and says it needs to be closed by the Lord. The second door is closed but he can feel a lot of good behind it and says, "It's really anointed in here and there is power, electromagnetic power."

• Participants all practice discerning.

• Paul continues and explains that the righteous power is being blocked so that there is no access to all that the Lord has for them. He asks the Lord what the legal right is for the evil door to be open. Then, with input from participants, it is determined to be negative influence, sexual perversion, religion, contempt for the Lord, and denying God.

• Paul shares, "I was at a conference as a speaker and was talking about Melchizedek, when the power of God fell in the room and people started experiencing the Lord. Then a man said, 'Oh! It's time for lunch, and we need to go to the next meeting', and he left. Poof! Like that! And you see, we have meetings in the church like that, where I want to teach them how to follow the Lord and not follow the program. I was an expert at the program, which is where we do things that we think need to be done, and ignore what the Lord wants to do. We have our 20 minutes of worship; we have the announcements and offering; we have the most important part, which is the sermon; and then we're gone. Right? I did that. It was like the longest hour of the week. But here, we come together and often don't even know what we are going to do. Before we know it the time has flown by."

• Discussion continues as one participant gives a prophetic word, another describes the vision he saw while she was speaking, and Paul determines that it is time to deal with the doors and gate.

• Paul says, "I do feel like the door that is shut is where things have been held back. So do we come together as a people of God and repent for following man rather than following God? Understand that when we talk about following man that it doesn't mean that we do not align ourselves with leadership, but that there's the attitude of not listening to the Lord. Do we repent for that? It is our desire to ask Jesus to close this door. Well, Jesus, we ask that You will close this door so it will never be opened again, and that You will have Your Kairos time invade every section of the grid. We ask Father, Son and Holy Spirit, that You will instruct the holy ones to issue a decree declaring this to be true."

• Paul puts his hands forward to discern and realizes that the gate is now open and there's a declaration written at the top.

• Participant says, "It seems like an infinity sign, and when you touched it, I felt evil that has gone on forever and repeats itself. Like these machines that keep moving and moving and moving? Perpetual machines. The rim of eternity or that part of eternity needs to be broken for this curse to go."

• Paul says, "Lord, we break the Greek mindset of ever-repeating cycles, and we declare that there is not a repeating cycle, that the Lord always moves in His time and is always moving to His new time and His new day, His new way. The Greeks perception of time is cyclical, but time is not cyclical in Hebrew. Time travels and moves.

• Participant says, "I think it's really important that it's the heart that's really the issue, and that's what it's all about. Eternity is written on the heart."

• Paul says, "That's from Ecclesiastes. Come here; you can feel that the gate is open; the door that was closed is open; and now the other door is good but is closed, and the evil is trapped behind it. Feel that? Feel how good it feels?"

• Participant says, "It feels like a breath."

• Paul reaches up with his right hand and says, "There is something written up here now that is very anointed."

• Participant reads, "All who are weary and seek rest."

• Paul responds, "That seems to be the theme. Rest. Entering into His rest. What was our part in this? It is that we agree with the Lord with what He wants us to do. That's our part. That's the battle. The battle is agreeing with the Lord. That's the battle. Actually, there's a flow of anointing coming out of this and it feels like time is coming back into right alignment."

CHAPTER THIRTEEN

Practicing Exploration

This chapter is a transcript from September 27, 2014, when Paul shared some new insights regarding the opening and closing of doors and gates during a Biblical Discernment and Exploration session.

As I have progressed in discernment, the Lord is always doing something new and there are times when He accentuates something. It's like, "Paul you need to pay attention to this." In this case I was in my Jacuzzi a couple of days ago when it felt like someone took an ice pick and jabbed me in my ear. I do have a tendency to develop ear infections so I thought that perhaps I was getting one because the pain was way down deep in the ear. While contemplating this, it happened 2 or 3 more times.

The next day I was on a Skype appointment with someone in Minnesota and it started to happen again, so as I often do in the midst of a session when I don't understand what's happening, I called someone for help. As we all discerned and discussed together, I realized I was discerning Jehovah Jireh. Now, on the way here today, I've just realized that I discern Jehovah Jireh in the same way that I feel Jesus' righteousness, so there seems to be a tie between Jehovah Jireh and righteousness.

In years gone by when I was pastoring a church, I would always be totally prepared when I began to teach or preach. But that was before I started doing what I'm doing now, because when we come together to study the Bible, the Lord just keeps giving new revelation regarding its meaning, and He often does the most unexpected things. But let's go ahead and look at the account in Genesis where Abraham has been told to offer Isaac as a sacrifice. It is very clear that Isaac was an adult man by now, which makes this an amazing act of submission of a son to his father.

> *Then they came to the place of which God had told him. And Abraham built an altar there and placed the wood in order; and he bound Isaac his son and laid him on the altar, upon the wood. And Abraham stretched out his hand and took the knife to slay his son. But the Angel of the LORD called to him from heaven and said, "Abraham, Abraham!" So he said, "Here I am." And He said, "Do not lay your hand on the lad, or do anything to him; for now I know that you fear God, since you have not withheld your son, your only son, from Me." Then Abraham lifted his eyes and looked, and there behind him was a ram caught in a thicket by its horns. So Abraham went and took the ram, and offered it up for a burnt offering instead of his son. And Abraham called the name of the place, The-LORD-Will-Provide; as it is said to this day, "In the Mount of the LORD it shall be provided."* [1]

The-Lord-Will-Provide is Jehovah Jireh, which we recognize as a very familiar name of the Lord. But, let's go on:

> *Then the Angel of the LORD called to Abraham a second time out of heaven, and said: "By Myself I have sworn, says the LORD, because you have done this thing, and have not withheld your son, your only son—blessing I will bless you, and multiplying I will multiply your descendants as the stars of the heaven and as the sand which is on the seashore; and your descendants shall possess the gate of their enemies."* [2]

So, look now at the Genesis account just after Rebekah had agreed to leave her family to accompany Abraham's servant to become Isaac's wife:

> *So they said, "We will call the young woman and ask her personally." Then they called Rebekah and said to her, "Will you go with this man?" And she said, "I will go." So they sent away Rebekah their sister and her nurse, and Abraham's servant and his men. And they blessed Rebekah and said to her: "Our sister, may you become the mother of thousands of ten thousands; and*

may your descendants possess the gates of those who hate them." [3]

So there are the gates!

As you came here today, you entered through a gate onto our property. Once inside, there are many doors, some of which may be closed and inaccessible without a key. Now think of the spiritual doors. If they are contaminated, there are bronze doors or iron bars, which means access to what God wants you to have is prohibited because they're closed. So the key is to find out why they are closed and take care of that, and then you have the full River of God. You lift up your gates so the King of Glory will come in, and not just come in but so He can come in and out. Now let's go back to Jehovah Jireh.

This all pertains somehow I think. Jehovah Jireh, as we have been taught previously, means the LORD will provide. But I looked it up in the Hebrew, and that is not as close as we need to get to see what really happens. The word actually means the LORD sees and He acts upon what He sees. So we know the LORD always sees, but the question for us has been why He doesn't appear to act upon what He is seeing. We pray, "Lord, I am in this mess right now. I don't feel good, I am not happy, and why don't You do something about it?" But here we have evidence that Jehovah Jireh does see, and He acts upon what He sees. With Isaac, the LORD sees that Abraham was obedient, and He sees that He does not want Abraham to offer up Isaac as the sacrifice. So He acts and provides a solution. The LORD sees, He acts upon it, and He provides a solution.

CHAPTER FOURTEEN

Making It Practical

One of our ongoing concerns is how to bring spiritual revelation into the practicality of our everyday lives, and Rob Gross models it well for us. Following, in outline form, is the content of a PowerPoint presentation he prepared for his church:

I. **Possessing the Gates:**

    A. The blessed life is that we have victory over the gates and doors of evil:

        1. *Blessing I will bless you, and multiplying I will multiply your descendants as the stars of the heaven and as the sand which is on the seashore; and your descendants shall possess the gate of their enemies.*[1]

    B. Who are the seed (the offspring) of the descendants of Abraham? We are![2]

        1. We are supposed to possess the gates of our enemies. To possess the gates means that we can overcome evil (trauma, sickness and death)!

        2. The mystery or secret of possessing the gates of our enemies (all forms of evil) is so important that the Lord revealed it to the generation that followed Abraham:

81

      a. *May your descendants possess the gates of those who hate them.[3]*

3. Why? Because God wants us to know that through Christ our enemies have been defeated.
4. Why? So we can set the captives free.
5. Why? So we can lead them to Jesus.

C. Jewish fathers pray Gen 24:60 over their daughters every week!

D. In the Bible, miracles happen at the gate!

II. Miracle at Your Gate:

A. *Now it happened, the day after, that He went into a city called Nain; and many of His disciples went with Him, and a large crowd. And when He came near the gate of the city, behold, a dead man was being carried out, the only son of his mother; and she was a widow. And a large crowd from the city was with her. When the Lord saw her, He had compassion on her and said to her, "Do not weep." Then He came and touched the open coffin, and those who carried him stood still. And He said, "Young man, I say to you, arise." So he who was dead sat up and began to speak. And He presented him to his mother. Then fear came upon all, and they glorified God, saying, "A great prophet has risen up among us"; and, "God has visited His people." And this report about Him went throughout all Judea and all the surrounding region.[4]*

B. *The battle is at the gate.[5]*

C. There are gates and doors all over your body:
1. Cells and molecules in the natural serve as gates and doors into different areas of the human body.
2. Gates and doors in the spiritual realms were established in the heavenly places by the enemy at the Fall, and later solidified through rebellion and generational iniquity.

D. We are connected to the heavenly places:
1. *Before I formed you in the womb I knew you; before you were born I sanctified you; I ordained you a prophet to the nations. [6]*
2. *...and raised us up together, and made us sit together in the heavenly places in Christ Jesus. [7]*

E. We are multi-dimensional: existing in time, space, height, width, and depth.

F. Gates and doors in the heavenly places keep people captive or imprisoned:

1. Inner hurts—depression, hopelessness, jealousy, rejection, shame, etc.

2. Physical diseases and chronic conditions—cancer, diabetes, heart, back, etc.

3. Spiritual torment—inability to sleep, fear, guilt, trauma, etc.

III. Jesus has given us keys to open the gates of inner hurts, physical sickness and trauma:

A. *...on this rock I will build my church, and the gates of Hades will not overcome it. I will give you the keys of the kingdom of heaven; whatever you bind on earth will be bound in heaven, and whatever you loose on earth will be loosed in heaven.*[8]

B. *The Spirit of the Lord is upon Me, because He has anointed Me to preach the gospel to the poor; He has sent Me to heal the brokenhearted, to proclaim liberty to the captives and recovery of sight to the blind, to set at liberty those who are oppressed.*[9]

IV. Gates & Doors:

A. *Thus says the Lord to his anointed, to Cyrus, whose right hand I have grasped, to subdue nations before him and to loose the belts of kings, to open doors before him that gates may not be closed: "I will go before you and level the exalted places, I will break in pieces the doors of bronze and cut through the bars of iron.*[10]

B. *Let them thank the Lord for his steadfast love, for his wondrous works to the children of man! For he shatters the doors of bronze and cuts in two the bars of iron.*[11]

V. How do we possess the gates?

A. *Enter into His gates with thanksgiving, and into His courts with praise. Be thankful to Him, and bless His name.*[12]

B. By first entering the double bronze doors.[13]

C. By unsealing the places that have been sealed because of the Fall, rebellion, and generational iniquity.

D. By making the crooked paths straight.

E. By opening all the righteous doors (when the double bronze doors are opened the gate cannot be shut) and asking the King of Glory to come through the gate.

F.   By smashing the double bronze doors and cutting the iron bars.

VI.   **What happens when the double bronze doors are opened and the gate cannot be shut?**

A.   *I will give you the treasures of darkness and hidden riches of secret places, that you may know that I, the Lord, who call you by your name, am the God of Israel.*[14]

VII.   **What happens when the crooked paths are made straight and the rough places are made smooth?**

A.   *The voice of one crying in the wilderness: "Prepare the way of the Lord; make straight in the desert a highway for our God. Every valley shall be exalted and every mountain and hill brought low; the crooked places shall be made straight and the rough places smooth; the glory of the Lord shall be revealed, and all flesh shall see it together; for the mouth of the Lord has spoken."* [15]

VIII. **We must not formularize the revelation of the gates and doors, but must follow Jesus' example:**

A.   *Then Jesus answered and said to them, "Most assuredly, I say to you, the Son can do nothing of Himself, but what He sees the Father do; for whatever He does, the Son also does in like manner.*[16]

IX.   **How do you know that the gates and doors are present on a person's body?**

A.   You may feel a sensation on a specific part of your body that is a gate on their body.

B.   You may place your hand over the gate to discern it on their body.

C.   By seeing the gate with your spiritual eyes.

X.   **How do you remove doors & gates? Re-read Isaiah 40:3-5 and 45:1-3, and pray them.**

CHAPTER FIFTEEN

From the Simple to the Complex

As we progress in our understanding of doors and gates, the Lord is leading us from the simple to the more complex. Just when we begin to think we understand what He has shown us, He reveals that we have only discerned the fundamentals of the revelation thus far. Simply put, we are still in preschool in terms of our understanding of the heavenly places. The good news is that even in our simplistic understanding, He is releasing healing to those for whom we pray. How much more healing will we see as the revelation increases?

Discernment of the doors and gates seems easy at first. If I (Paul) put my hand in front of me I can feel the door or gate. If I turn my hand in an opposite direction in the same space I do not feel anything. If you have seen the film, *Voyage of the Dawn Treader,* you may remember that when Lucy was on the island she saw a door, but when she looked from the other side of the door she realized it could not be seen. This is exactly how I discern doors and gates. I ask the Lord if it is a gate or a door and I get an increase of pressure on my head regarding the correct one, which I call a 'hit', and then I know which one it is.

Initially, we were confused about the importance of knowing whether what we were feeling was a gate or door but the Lord has shown us that we must first correctly interpret the key scripture regarding gates and doors in Isaiah 45, as indicated previously. After several months, it became clear that when we dealt with evil tied to the doors, the closed gate would be opened. Previously, we had tried to open the gates but were unsuccessful until we learned that the doors in the dimensions must be handled first.

When I feel the door I can immediately tell if it is good or evil. It took a considerably longer time to realize that this discernment was not sufficient in dealing with the doors. I would feel beyond the door and know whether what was behind it was good or evil. It then occurred to me that if what was behind the door was evil, the door was really open and was affecting either me or someone else. If what I felt behind the door was anointed and of God, then that door was closed.

The Lord led us to look at generational issues that gave the enemy a right to use the evil behind that door to affect the person. After renouncing and repenting for those issues, we noticed that the evil door would be closed. We then asked the Lord to open the righteous doors that had been closed. When this was accomplished, I could discern that the gate that had been closed was now also opened. We did not need to deal with any issues of the gates—it happened by default, which is exactly what is stated in Isaiah 45:1 (ESV), *"to open doors before him, that gates may not be closed."*

Jesus then reminded us that He has the keys for the doors. As was explained in *Heaven Trek,* the Lord had shown us the importance of Isaiah 22:22. Eliakim, a priest, replaces the imposter Shebna and receives the key of David. Then Eliakim, now a King Priest, is allowed to open that which can no longer be shut, and to close that which can no longer be opened. As is clear from the succeeding verses, at this point Eliakim walks in amazing favor. We are then told, in Revelation 3:7-8, that Jesus has received this key of David and what He shuts no one can open, and what He opens no one can shut. We often acknowledge this fact in our prayers about the doors, reminding the enemy that he must give up the keys to Jesus, and we then ask Jesus to open and close doors. This scripture clearly states that once this is done, all doors that have been closed or opened cannot be opened or shut again. It would appear that this is a permanent solution to the generational issue that has been prayed through.

In February of 2014, we hosted our annual Aslan's Place Summit. After discussing doors and gates we decided to apply what we had learned. A couple that has been in ministry for many years was suffering continued financial hardship. We had them sit at the front of the room, and asked the Lord to show us the doors that were blocking them from the resources they needed, both to live their lives and to bless the ministry to which they were assigned. Not only did we discern doors, but also an attic and a mirror at the end of a corridor that camouflaged a hidden door behind the mirror. After an extended prayer time, all the doors that we perceived needed to be closed or opened were taken care of. Now it was time to see if what we had done in the heavenly places actually affected their lives here on Earth.

It did! They went home, and within weeks a door opened for them to move to another city, and they moved from an apartment to a wonderful small house in a beautiful city. After moving, the woman was hired to be an administrative assistant. At the present time they have not yet seen complete victory in their finances, but they have definitely seen amazing progress.

In 2011, when Donna and I were on a book tour, Paul Knight[1] from London, England, joined us in Minnesota. While teaching on the gates and doors, I was showing how they are tied to our physical body, using a participant as an example. I had previously discerned that if there were a problem in a certain part of the body, I would feel an ungodly gate or door there. I showed how each gate and each door seem to actually be spiritual beings called stars, making them star gates and star doors. I could feel a line coming off of that point on the body, and as I followed that line in the Spirit, I found what seemed to be a sphere. That sphere seemed to be a door. Now I was confused. How was it that I had felt doors like one would feel a door in the natural, but now I felt a door as a sphere? Now the complexity begins.

When we are discerning dimensionally, we really are discerning from our three dimensions what is actually in much higher dimension(s). Therefore, we are interpreting a multi-dimensional place within the confines of three dimensions. The Apostle Paul reminds us in 1 Corinthians 13:12 that we only see in part. As we progress, we will see that what appears to be a flat door or gate is really much more complex.

As I followed that line from the problem part in the body and felt the sphere, I could also feel three stars inside of the sphere (which was the door). I could feel and hear each of these stars and realized that these three stars seemed to be notes, and together they made up a musical cord. I asked Paul Knight, who is a composer in the theater district of London, to touch each note to sense the tone. He did, and then went to a keyboard and played the chord, which was actually a discord. I then noticed that one star seemed stronger than the other two stars. I discovered a line coming off of that star and as I followed that line I found another sphere, which also contained a chord of three stars. Paul Knight discerned that chord, played it, and again it was a discord. He said that the stronger note I felt in the first sphere was a transition note to the chord in the second sphere.

Next, I discerned that there was also a stronger note in the second sphere, and followed the line coming off of that note. Expecting to feel another sphere I was surprised to discern a series of seven stars. Through revelation, we felt the Lord was saying this was the spiritual 'seven sisters', or Pleiades,[2] but at this time we do not yet understand the significance of Pleiades. We have discovered that the two spheres seem to be tied to our mother and father, and are an indication of a bondage that prohibits us from leaving the sphere of influence of our parents. We also can clearly see that these gates and doors are all tied to star trek, star gates, and star wars.

As we were praying, the Lord had us close all the ungodly doors and disconnect from all ungodly spiritual stars. The Lord also had us pray for other issues. That night, the person we had prayed for slept the entire night for the first time she could remember. More tangible results!

CHAPTER SIXTEEN

Testimonies of Change

An email from Heather Baker to Paul Cox:

> Yesterday I was watching your Star Wars seminar on YouTube. You
> had been talking about the grid and intersections and the gates and
> doors. I have been able to see the grid since hearing the first talk.
>
> I have been on disability for four and one-half months with pain in
> my hip and spine. The hip was resolved less than 1 month ago. The
> orthopedist discovered two degenerated discs, 1 herniated disc, and
> a bunch of other abnormalities on my spine. Last Wednesday I had
> an epidural into the herniated disc. This relieved about 50% of my
> pain. I was so thankful.
>
> Yesterday, while I was listening to your Star Wars talks, I got up to
> move and fold laundry, as staying in one position for too long has
> been very painful.

I asked the Lord if there was a gate related to my back pain. Immediately I saw a hatch opening up on my back. It was about the size of a large ventilation/heating duct. I went in. I saw the stars and heavens. At the end of the tunnel I got out and walked a few paces on the heavens. Then I realized I could not take one more step before falling off an infinite cliff of some sort. Beyond the cliff and downwards were things that looked like the nebulae they show on *Star Trek/Star Wars*. But there was nothing I could walk on, even though I had been previously walking on what looked like space.

I asked the Lord what this place was, and He said it is the beginning of humanity. There were no humans around except me, so I was a bit confused. He said it was the conception of humanity. OK, so I stood there, making sure not to fall off the cliff. Then I saw two beings: a gray lizard man, and a very tall black-robed being with black skin and very long fingers. Neither of them felt very good. I watched as the lizard man made a deal of some sort with the black robe being. I asked the Lord what was going on and who were these guys. He said the black-robed guy was the father of Death (I believe He meant initiator of Death), and the lizard man was an ancestor who looked like a lizard because he had made so many covenants with the serpent. I then realized the lizard ancestor man was making a deal about his future descendants, selling us out.

In Jesus' authority, I repented for and renounced the covenant lizard man was making with black robe guy, and poured the blood of Jesus on it, asking that the covenant be dissolved. Suddenly, the lizard man disintegrated. The black robe guy went walking on as though the event had never happened.

I stood there watching for a while, not knowing what to do. And then I thought I might as well fold the laundry while I am standing here. So when I reached out for something to fold, there was a clicking noise in my back, and the pain was much relieved.

The pain has remained reduced for about 18 hours now. There is still some, but that may be due to muscles needing strengthening.

From Rob Gross:

A retired man shared with me that his doctor had ordered a routine MRI of his chest. When the results came back, the doctor called him to say that the MRI revealed two dark spots on one of his lungs and further testing was needed immediately.

I asked the man if I could pray for him and he agreed. I held my hand in front of his chest and discerned a bronze door. I then asked the Lord to open the bronze door so the gates would no longer be shut, and for Him to pull down every exalted place in the man's generational line. I then closed the prayer by asking the Lord to release His healing glory into the man's lungs.

The man visited his physician that week for additional testing. Two weeks later, he called to inform me that his doctor had called him to let him know that the follow up testing revealed that the dark spots had completely disappeared!

Barbara Parker's Experience:

After a Saturday workshop, several of us decided to go to a movie. Throughout the day I had a toothache on the right side of my mouth that was steadily getting worse. As we headed for the car, I complained to Paul that I didn't know how I could take it much longer. He discerned unrighteous doors that were open, said a quick prayer to close them and open the righteous ones, and we got in the car. As Paul began driving, my right jaw started getting numb just like it would if a dentist had injected Lidocaine, and within a few minutes I couldn't feel anything. The numbness persisted for several hours and when it disappeared most of the pain was gone as well. On Monday, I called for a dental appointment, but it was several days before they could see me, by which time all of my symptoms were gone. The dentist could see where there was still a small opening through which an abscess had drained. I'll take the Lord's way of doing a dental procedure any day over a trip to the dentist!

CHAPTER SEVENTEEN
Traveling in Heavenly Places

In November 2011, Rob Gross and I (Paul) were in Hong Kong. We had returned to our hotel after a day of ministry and were enjoying a meal at a wonderful restaurant just off of the lobby. Suddenly I felt a pressure on my head and realized I did not know what I was discerning. The Lord was doing something new. Rob then joined me in asking the Lord what we were feeling. After posing a series of questions to the Lord, He revealed that we were sensing Michael, the archangel. I then heard in my spirit, Daniel 12:1. My first reaction was, "There is nothing about Michael the archangel in Daniel 12," but I looked up the scripture and, to my surprise, Michael is mentioned there:

> *At that time Michael shall stand up,*
> *The great prince who stands watch over the sons of your people;*
> *And there shall be a time of trouble,*
> *Such as never was since there was a nation,*
> *Even to that time.*
> *And at that time your people shall be delivered,*

Every one who is found written in the book.

This would not be the first time Rob and I would discern Michael.

Some years ago the Lord had given me the discernment of the archangel Gabriel when, with a teenager in the San Francisco area, we were visiting some local sights. Unexpectedly, I felt a pressure on two parts of the left side of the back of my head. I asked the Lord out loud what I was now discerning, and the teenager responding by saying, "The Lord just said you are discerning Gabriel, the archangel."

We find Gabriel mentioned not only in the annunciation passage in Luke but also in Daniel. In Daniel 8:16 and Daniel 9:21 Gabriel is said to bring interpretation, or understanding, to what Daniel had seen. The name Gabriel means 'man of God' or 'strength of God'.[1] We were to discover that both Michael and Gabriel have other functions as well.

We come together monthly at Aslan's Place for Biblical Discernment Explorations. For several years we had a youth group that met weekly, until it was disbanded in the spring of 2014. I also travel to many places and conduct meetings. At all of these events it has now become commonplace to discern either Michael or Gabriel and, because of previous encounters with them, I know that we are being taken somewhere in the heavenly places. We have learned that we are not discerning Michael or Gabriel being with us in our physical location, but rather that we are traveling with them. At times I have felt only one of them, but at other times we seem to travel with both.

Such experiences begin with us waiting somewhere in the heavenly places. Many individuals have seen what appears to be a waiting room with round couches. This literally is 'waiting on the Lord'. We then can feel movement, and know we are being taken someplace. Some have seen us riding on the backs of Michael or Gabriel, and when both are involved, we are often tossed back and forth between the archangels as we travel.

Eventually we stop traveling and discern that the Lord has taken us to a gate someplace in the heavenly places where He indicates that He wants us to take care of the problem with that gate. We follow the model previously written about in this book. We check inside of the gate and determine how many doors are present, which doors are open and which ones are closed. Through the guidance of the Holy Spirit, we seek understanding about the nature of the gate and doors—what the issue is, and what we are to do in generational prayer to release the stronghold on the doors so the righteous doors can be opened and the gates released. Once the gates are open, the glory of God and the river of God can flow freely in and out of those gates.

A recent experience illustrates this process. In February 2015, I was leading a coaching session for three individuals in Pittsburg, Pennsylvania when I found myself in a new spiritual location. A participant said she saw us in the library in Heaven, specifically within a vault in the library. I recognized that I was discerning something new, and identified the sensation on my head as the heavenly library.

We were traveling again, but this time it was not with Gabriel or Michael. I discerned that the Captain of the Host[2] and the host[3] were present. They took us to a different place in the ungodly depth and I could discern that there was a contaminated gate, which was located in the darkness.[4] The Lord revealed that this gate has blocked our access to the heavenly library and to the revelation He has for us there. As we explored why this was possible, we realized that this issue went all the way back to Adam and Eve. Because there was no fear of the Lord, the first couple ignored dependence on God, deciding instead to choose their own way and make their own plans. At that point the access to the library was blocked, and that iniquity has traveled down our generational lines.

Wondering, "After all the generational deliverance we've done, what is there left to pray?" So we petitioned the Lord saying, "Lord, we need your help to remove the blockages that are prohibiting the gate from being opened." Instantly, we were back in the heavenly library and the heavenly librarian handed us a book. Its title, *The Book of Wisdom,* was written in gold on the cover. We asked the Lord to open the book and read to us how to get out of this darkness so we could access the plans in the heavenly library, admitting that without Him we could do nothing. The librarian then walked back to Jesus, Who was standing there next to us. He showed the Lord something, and we asked, "What is the librarian showing You?" The response came before we finished the question, "You are the Way, the Truth, and the Life and no one comes to the Father without You." [5]

Immediately, I felt the host warring in the heavenly places and we began traveling again, back into the darkness. The sense of evil was horrible in this place. We prayed:

Jesus, we ask You to come and shine Your light here, we welcome You to come, and we declare that You have all the keys. We ask now that You open this gate, for we desire to have access to Your plans and dreams for us.

The gate opened and the Lord gave us access.

Over the past three years we have been taken to many heavenly places in the length, width, height and depth. He has showed us many gates that are contaminated and has identified the doors that need to be touched for the sake of His Kingdom. We believe that each of our family lines has their own sphere of influence, and in these spheres there are many contaminated gates and doors that need attention. When we exercise our authority in Christ as revealed sons of God, taking back these places that have been captured by the enemy, we will experience levels of freedom and victory we never dreamed possible.

More importantly, the Lord is using us to establish His Kingdom on Earth. This is the great joy that we have as kings and priests of the Most High God. We are warriors in the Kingdom and we will not hold back until His Kingdom is fully established. We will not hesitate to do our part under the Lordship of our warrior King. The Kingdom of God has suffered violence but we are violently taking it back in agreement with scripture:

> *The kingdom of heaven suffers violence, and the violent take it back.*[6]

CHAPTER EIGHTEEN

Looking Ahead

This volume was essentially finished and released for editing when more information was received, which seems to point to the future in terms of an increased understanding of gates and doors. Our Lord has so much more for us to understand, and a good analogy would be that so far we've just dipped our toes into the vast oceans of His wisdom, knowledge and understanding.

Dawn Bray and Jana Green had been together on Skype, and had discerned and done some work on a gate. The following day, Dawn became very sick with what appeared to be an attack that included a violent attack on her stomach. While lying in bed, the Lord showed her several things:

> I saw the grid with red stars or lights and, at different times, white stars or lights. I think they were about the star gates and star wars.

> I saw faces of witches and warlocks as well as horses running toward me. When close enough, I could see the horses had the face of a man with long hair that had looked like a mane from a distance. Were they Centaurs or Kentauroi?[1] It feels like it could be related to Pleiades and the two spheres still being unpacked.

> I felt Elijah's spirit and heard the words, "gate of demise." Asking the Lord about that, He said that Elijah came into agreement with the gate of demise when he ran from Jezebel.

My dad's spirit/his face came to me in a vision that caused light to flash around me and I began to see 'turn around'. For context, the last time I had this kind of experience was about four years ago, when my grandmother came to me in a vision and a turn around began (my dad was still alive at that time).

I heard the phrase, "The loophole the enemy used will be the noose that hangs him."

The following day I was resting and soaking to regain strength, when I had a vision of Jesus coming to me. He knelt down beside me and began to weep. He placed His hands on my stomach and then bent across me. I asked why He was weeping and He replied, "Because I paid the price for all to receive, but you haven't been able to receive." I felt His compassion and His desire to give us everything—to give us victory—in that moment. He is determined for us to have it all!

He picked me up in the vision, carried me to the Garden of Gethsemane, and showed me the struggle for what He called 'perfect love'. Then He carried me to the foot of the cross. He was on the cross and I was there at the foot of the cross like Mary would have been. I listened, as Jesus as the Son of Man, became perfect love so that we could receive the keys and be revealed as sons of God.

At the same moment, I saw a flash of timelines from the crucifixion to the resurrection—the torn veil, the grave, going into hell and holding the keys, the resurrection and ascension—which created a sound that I knew was the sound of the blood of Jesus. I don't quite know how else to put that in words. I said, "Jesus, You have the keys," and He said, "YOU have the keys because I am in you." I felt waves of His love and the glory washing over me, and knew that it was in intimacy and identity that we will learn the next steps to possess the gates. Then I received this message:

> There are gateways
> There are doors
> The enemy cannot afford
> To lose control, to give them over
> He used the branch of both father and mother

When through THE Power[2]
You gain control
All oppression will have to go
You have the plan
You have the key
It's hidden in your identity
When who you are is all of Me
My perfect love will help you see
Possess the gates
Possess the courts
The power struggle until he aborts (the enemy)
The mission is clear
The time is present
Don't let the enemy have the gates
Don't relent
In perfect love I overcame
And all this power play is like a game
8's on the front
8's on the back
8's on the chessboard
8's to attack
There is a frequency
There is a sound
There is a resonance
That's not been found
To reverse the plan
To dismantle the hidden
Collect at the gate
Where all is forgiven

I saw a portal over the vision I had seen as Jesus ascended, which was a gate; and I also was aware that there could be a gate releasing a sound at the blood of Abel.

> *But you have come to Mount Zion and to the city of the living God, the heavenly Jerusalem, to an innumerable company of angels, to the general assembly and church of the firstborn who are registered in heaven, to God the Judge of all, to the spirits of just men made perfect, to Jesus the Mediator of the new covenant, and to the blood of sprinkling that*

speaks better things than that of Abel.[3]

And being in agony, He prayed more earnestly. Then His sweat became like great drops of blood falling down to the ground.[4]

A short time later, the revelation continued in a prayer session when a gate with two lines or connections was discerned. In Dawn's words:

> One line went up, was connected to three bright stars, and had a green nebula appearance around it. The Lord showed us it was part of Orion's belt. I had seen the horse with the man's face and hair previously so I looked it up later. It was from the constellation Sagittarius (but without the bow and arrow in my vision). The three stars were called either the three sisters or the three kings, and make up the belt of the Hunter.

> The second line or connection went down, and we discerned it was to the ungodly depth. I immediately thought of Job 38:31:

> *Can you bind the cluster of the Pleiades, or loose the belt of Orion?*

> I also realized that as I had seen the white stars and the red stars previously, the bluish white and red stars are called super giants (the most massive and luminous stars). Also, Orion, in Babylonian, was called the heavenly shepherd (the chief God of the heavenly realms).

> We prayed some things and felt that Father disconnected her and the gate shifted, and we were not sure if one gate left and another one came or if the gate was cleansed, but it even shifted to a different place in my discernment. I really don't understand this but feel like it is something to unpack.

> I also feel like there is a connection to the possessing the gates of those who hate us related to jealousy in the body of Christ in general that is stopping forward movement for many. I have definitely fought this in my journey and have a testimony that I think is linked to breaking this cycle.

> I was with my ministry teams and we received an angelic message, after which one of the men felt he was to pray and push back some

things. As he prayed, the Lord showed me in the Spirit that this was a picture of doing business at the gate, and what he decreed was upheld by the rulers, holy ones and watchers. We took back and/or possessed a gate of our enemy through the message, the prayer and the decrees. This is where it gets really exciting.

Is this answer to prayer for the fruit? I had been praying (as well as others) about a release of favor to see a standard in our fellowship that requires those who lead and minister to others to go through healing prayer ministry as part of their training and equipping process. The Lord has shown me His heart for this fellowship to become a healing hub for those who will come in and need healing (the harvest), and His heart for the intimacy and healing necessary to walk in the freedom to fulfill the vision. On Wednesday (the following day), I received a phone call from a new member to our leadership team. He had met with our Pastor that morning and then contacted me to inquire about setting up a program to put this requirement in place for his team. I was surprised as he shared his heart. It was the same thing the Lord had shown me previously, and I had been praying for this several years as the leader of the healing rooms and suddenly it broke open! I felt the breakthrough was directly related to possessing the gate the night before. WOW! I love this stuff!!

It's always wonderful to observe how God confirms His words! If you recall, we were praying at Paul's house in January 2011, when the revelation about the gates really began in earnest. The gates that were discerned had been enabled by gossip (which was motivated by jealousy), and it seemed to have to do with forward or backward directions. Additionally, Dawn's picture of doing business in the gates is right in line with the previous discussion of the legal significance of gates.

I (Barbara) love it when God brings us full circle, and often notice that is exactly what happens when I'm facilitating Spirit-led discussions and He ties the ending thought right back to the beginning. And so it appears that He's done it again, in this case providing a final chapter after we thought the book was finished that not only confirms our journey but also promises more to come!

ENDNOTES

Introduction

1   Matthew 6:9–13
2   Luke19:44
3   Matthew 23:13

Chapter 1: *Highways to Holiness*

1   An airline pilot who, in hundreds of miles of flying, observed many UFOs, but especially noticed that the UFOs followed certain routes, developed the World Grid computer program. His observation and the observation of other pilots led him into a scientific and mathematical study of a magnetic worldwide grid—a scientific confirmation of the grid. http://www.worldgrid.net/products/gridpoint-atlas/

2   Persis Tiner is a minister and prophetic intercessor. She is a board member of Joel's Well Ministries.

3   Larry Pearson is a co-founder of Lion Sword Communications. He is a co-founder and board member of Joel's Well Ministries. His website is http://www.lionsword.ca

Chapter 2: *Introducing the Grid*

1   Dale Shannon is a professional life coach, professor and minister. Her website is http://fulfillyourdream.org

2   Rob Gross is the pastor of Mountain View Community Church in Kaneohe, Hawaii, and is co-author of *Exploring Heavenly Places, Volume II, Revealing the sons of God.*

3   Acts 1:8
4   Romans 1:16 KJV
5   Romans 8:11
6   Romans 15:18-19 ESV
7   1 Corinthians 1:18 KJV
8   1 Corinthians 2:3-4 ESV
9   1 Corinthians 2:5 KJV
10 1 Corinthians 4:20
11 1 Thessalonians 1:5 ESV
12 Isaiah 35:8 ESV
13 Matthew 3:1-3 ESV
14 Matthew 10:5-8 ESV
15 Genesis 22:17 ESV
16 Genesis 24:60 ESV

17   Genesis 28:17 ESV

18   John 1:51 ESV

29   Isaiah 62:10 ESV

20   Psalm 24:7 ESV

21   Proverbs 8:34 NIV

Chapter 3: *Ongoing Revelation of the Grid*

1   More information about powers is included in *Come up Higher* by Paul L. Cox.

2   Jana Green is an artist, a minister, and a prophetic intercessor. Her website is http://www.signsandwondersstudio.com

3   Lewis Crompton is a marketplace minister and a board member of Joel's Well ministries. His website is http://keybearerministries.com

4   Mimi Lowe is a minister, an author, and a member of the board of Joel's Well Ministries. Her website is http://www.mimilowe.com

5   Dena Plantage is a prayer minister and bookstore manager at Aslan's Place.

6   Ephesians 6:10-13

7   Dawn Bray is a prayer minister and prophetic intercessor. Her website is http://newreflectionministries.org

Chapter 4: *Testimonials About the Grid*

1   Heather Baker's ministry is the South Bay House of Prayer in Torrance, CA

2   Kelly Stark served as a missionary in Romania for 15 years, and is the author of *The Darkest Places*. She currently lives in Southern California with her four adopted Romanian children.

Chapter 5: *A Confirming Vision*

1   Isaiah 11:9b-10 KJV

2   See Isaiah 55:11

Chapter 6: *Introducing the Doors*

1   http://en.wikipedia.org/wiki/I_Hear_You_Knocking

2   Deuteronomy 31:6

3   Revelation 3:20

4   John 10:9

5   http://www.thefreedictionary.com/door

Chapter 7: *Introducing the Gates*

1   Psalm 24:7-10
2   http://www.merriam-webster.com/medical/gate
3   Genesis 28:17, Job 17:16, Job 38:17, Psalm 107:18, Psalm 118:19-20, Matthew 16:18, Revelation 21
4   Deuteronomy 3:5
5   Nehemiah 2:7-8
6   Exodus 27:16 KJV, 38:18
7   1 Kings 23:8
8   2 Kings 23:8-9
9   Psalm 100:4
10 Proverbs 8:34
11 Amos 5:15
12 Zechariah 8:16
13 Matthew 7:13-14
14 Proverbs 22:22-23
15 Deuteronomy 29:12; Isaiah 57:2; Matthew 25:21,23
16 Lamentations 2:9
17 Hebrews 13:12
18 Isaiah 3:26a
19 Isaiah 14:31
20 Jeremiah 14:2
21 Psalm 24:7-10

Chapter 8: *Earthly and Heavenly Gates*

1   John 10:27
2   Ezekiel 44:1-2
3   http://www.katapi.org.uk/Maps/Jerusalem400.htm
4   There are additional references for the gates of the temple that are not noted here.
5   Nehemiah 3:1, 32; 12:39; John 5:2
6   2 Chronicles 33:14; Nehemiah 3:3, 12:39; Zephaniah 1:10
7   Nehemiah 3:6, 12:39
8   2 Chronicles 26:9; Nehemiah 2:13, 3:13
9   Nehemiah 3:13-14, 12:31; Jeremiah 19:2
10 http://www.therain.org/appendixes/app59.html
11 Nehemiah 3:15, 12:37
12 Nehemiah 3:26, 8:3; 12:37
13 Nehemiah 3:28; Jeremiah 31:40
14 Nehemiah 3:29

15 Nehemiah 3:31

16 2 Kings 14:13, 2 Chronicles 25:23, Nehemiah 8:16, 12:39

17 2 kings 11:6,19; Nehemiah 12:39; Acts 12:10

18 2 Kings 14:13; 2 Chronicles 25:23, 26:9; Jeremiah 31:38; Zechariah 14:10

19 Jeremiah 20:2, 37:13, 38:7; Ezekiel 48:32; Zechariah 14:10

20 Zechariah 14:10

21 Joshua 8:29; 2 Kings 23:8

22 2 Chronicles 23:5

23 Matthew 16:18

24 Job 17:15-16

Chapter 9: *Legal Significance of Gates*

1 Deuteronomy 16:18

2 Deuteronomy 21:19

3 Ruth 4:1

4 Joshua 8:29

5 1 Samuel 4:18

6 Judges 18:17

7 Joshua 6:26 and 1 Kings 16:34

8 Deuteronomy 14:29

9 Deuteronomy 15:17

10 Deuteronomy 31:12

11 Deuteronomy 23:15-16

12 Deuteronomy 24:14

13 Deuteronomy 28:52

14 Judges 16:2

15 http://en.wikipedia.org/wiki/Janus

16 Details regarding how to deal with gates will be shared in detail in successive chapters. At this point, we were just beginning to learn what to do with gates and ongoing revelation clarified things immensely.

Chapter 10: *Open and Closed Gates and Doors*

1 Psalm 24:7

2 Isaiah 45:1-2 NKJV

3 Psalm 107:16 NKJV

4 Isaiah 45:1-2 ESV

5 Psalm 107:16 ESV

Chapter 12: *Practicing Discernment*

---

1   See January 11, 2014, and September 27, 2014, at http://aslansplace.com/august-9th-2014-sessions-of-biblical-discernment-exploration/

Chapter 13: *Practicing Exploration*

---

1   Genesis 22:9-14
2   Genesis 22:15-17
3   Isaiah 24:57-60

Chapter 14: *Making It Practical*

---

1   Genesis 22:17
2   Galatians 3:29
3   Genesis 24:60
4   Luke 7:11-17
5   Isaiah 28:6
6   Jeremiah 1:5
7   Ephesians 2:6
8   Matthew 16:18-19 NIV
9   Luke 4:18
10   Isaiah 45:1-2 ESV
11   Psalm 107:8, 19 ESV
12   Psalm 100:4
13   The Hebrew is actually 'doors' and not double doors, and the bronze doors and iron bars seem to be the contamination of the righteous doors. Godly doors are covered up by the bronze and iron.
14   Isaiah 45:3
15   Isaiah 40:3-5
16   John 5:19

Chapter 15: *From the Simple to the Complex*

---

1   Paul Knight is a composer in the theater district in London, England. With his wife, Jan, he oversees Aslan's Place, London, and is also a member of the Board of Directors of Joel's Well Ministries.
2   Job 9:9, 38:31, Amos 5:8

Chapter 17: *Traveling in Heavenly Places*

1   Wood, D. R. W., & Marshall, I. H. (1996). In *New Bible Dictionary* (3rd ed.). Leicester, England; Downers Grove, IL: InterVarsity Press.

2   Joshua 5:13-15. I believe the Captain of the Host is a created being and not the Lord. In Joshua 5:14, we are told that Joshua bowed down and worshipped but the text does not say that Joshua worshipped the Captain of the Host. The Hebrew word for 'captain' is *sar* and is translated in other passages as 'prince'. In Daniel there is a reference to the prince of Persia and the prince of Greece. Jesus is the prince of princes. Note also that when Joshua asks the prince, "What does my Lord say to His servant" the word used is *adon* which means 'master', and can refer to men or God. In the phrase, "Commander of the Lord's Host," the word 'Lord' is 'Yahweh' which is clearly the Lord.

3   Many have seen the host as humanoid type spiritual warriors. The Captain of the Host is over this group. There also seem to be other host, thus the word host and host (plural) in the Old Testament. There is the humanoid type host, the angelic host, the starry host, the mighty ones host, the saint host and the living saint host.

4   Job 10:21

5   John 14:6

6   Matthew 11:12

Chapter 18: *Looking Ahead*

1   http://www.theoi.com/Georgikos/KentauroiThessalioi.html

2   Matthew 26:64

3   Hebrews 12:22-24

4   Luke 22:44

PERSONAL NOTES